SPIRALLING
DOWN
THE
RABBIT
HOLE
AND
ESCAPING
THROUGH
THE
LOOKING
GLASS

Revised Edition

Introduction

This anthology consists of a three-part trilogy of previously published books and are a personal mental health journey through ramblings and rhymes, from a secretive very dark existence to an openly less shady one.

This book is a memory box of thoughts and past memories, many of which have no useful value and should have been discarded long ago. Many have taken on a new life in written word form and have acquired their own flow or rhythm.

Although some of the subject matter is relevant to the experiences of younger children this book is intended for adolescent and adult reading.

Rambling Rhymes
Through Difficult Times...

...(*Eggs over easy!*)

Part I

Rambling Rhymes Through Difficult Times…

…(Eggs Over Easy!)

Struggling under the radar with anxiety, depression and suicidal thoughts from an early age, John begins using poetry to write down his spiralling thoughts. Often with a sense of dark humour and irony.

Eventually, John reaches a crisis point and events bring his mental health under the microscope, exposing his long-term inability to effectively control his emotional well-being.

John can no longer hide behind his mask!

Dedication

This anthology is dedicated
to
the memory of my best friend
and
anyone who has ever experienced mental health issues,
or had a positive effect on someone else's mental health.

Acknowledgements.

Thank you to…
Those of you who have listened, supported, encouraged and
afforded me their time and concern.
Especially those family and friends who took me under their wings
and ensured I went on long walks.
Anna, Claire, Connie, Da-Sheena, Gemma, Jenny, Lottie, Lucy,
Terence, Teresa and the family of my best friend, for their kind
permission to include the poems personal to them.
My daughter Gemma for proofreading my work and correcting
my grammar.
Our cats! We have always been 'owned' by cats and although some
have long since passed, they have always been wonderful company
and ongoing relaxation therapy.
A special acknowledgment to Stephen Fry, as without his inspiration
for the first steps to write these poems, they would not exist.

Rambling Rhymes Through Difficult Times…

…(Eggs over easy!)

**A collection of poems on a personal
mental health journey
through the light and shade**

Foreword.

My Personal Journey

This introduction and poems are my mental health journey. So probably the best way to explain why I have decided to publish these poems is to be honest and open on my journey so far, as below.

My journey started in what many still refer to as
'The Good Old Days!'

I was the second eldest of four children, born in 1961 to a single mother. My elder brother being my half-brother, having a different father to my younger brother, sister and I. In those days children born out of wedlock were called many things, but the technical legal term 'illegitimate' amuses me. It infers I was somehow born illegally or as a criminal, which is of course ridiculous.

My father was Polish and was already married with four children by his own wife. So, I have two full siblings and five half-related siblings. All eleven of us lived in a three bedroom house in the Semilong area of Northampton. My mother was the live-in-nurse to my father's wife, who was recovering from breast cancer. My father took advantage of the situation multiple times over many years, against the will of my mother. Hence, the arrival of my sister, younger brother and I.

My father was a very violent individual, whom I now presume suffered from Post-Traumatic Stress Disorder (PTSD), as a result of his wartime experiences in the Polish Resistance. I have been led to understand his two sisters were shot, because they would not give him up. He apparently also bore the scars of being shot several times, whilst fortunately escaping not only once, but twice following capture by the Nazi`s. He arrived in the UK towards the latter end of the war and although born in the USA, he was of Polish decent. He had no living relatives to return to, so stayed in the UK instead of returning home to the then Russian controlled Poland.

15

It seemed to me my father's wife brought me up as a child, until she died when I was 7 years old. In reality, it was because my mother had returned to full-time work and my father's wife took care of us in the daytime. Upon her death, I eventually realised the person who slept in the same bedroom as us, was actually my mother.

Not long after my father's wife's death, my mother left my father following more domestic violence episodes. Taking with her my sister 3 years old, younger brother 4 years old and myself 7 years old. Initially moving to my mother's friend's house also in the Semilong area. To this day, I remember carrying our bunk bed frames to our new address.

Sadly, due to my father's threatening behaviour towards my mother's friend, we had to move out after approximately a week. So, at this point my mother took us to the Police Station, effectively making us all homeless. We spent the whole of that Sunday on a long wooden bench in front of the Police Station reception. It seemed like the longest day of my life and still does.

Just before this event my elder brother, who was four years older than me, was placed in a children's home and eventually a borstal, due to attacking a female teacher at school. No real surprise in hindsight, as he had experienced my father's violent actions towards our mother and us as children, for much longer than I.

From this point in time and until he was 16 years old, my elder brother would only come home to stay at Christmas, Easter and Summer holidays. Social Services did make many attempts to put my younger brother, sister and I into care, but my mother refused to give us up.

Looking back, it was a very courageous thing for my mother to do in the 1960's. We had no further real contact with my father and four much older half- brothers from this point onwards, as my mother ensured we kept a low profile.

The fear of my father and the feel of the buckle end of a thick leather belt regularly, is something I will never forget as one of the main memories between the age of 4 and 7 years. Ironically, to be counterbalanced by the love and affection afforded to me by his wife, who still has a very special place in my memories.

The next three to four years we spent moving between different schools and temporary unsafe hostels/housing. Initially in a hostel on the corner of Kerr Street and the Upper Mounts, overlooking Campbell Square Police Station and The Mounts Fire Station in the centre of Northampton. All four of us living in just a single bedroom, whilst sharing bathroom and kitchen facilities with three other families. Followed by sharing a three-storey house between the Wellingborough and Kettering Road area of Northampton with another family. At this point it was not uncommon to be left babysitting my younger brother and sister in the evening until quite late from the age of 9 years old. A notable event at Market Street was my mother's foot coming through the ceiling during breakfast. After we moved out, the whole street was demolished.

We were housed in the Spencer Estate area of Northampton in 1971, when I was 10 years old. By this time, I was already cleaning the house, preparing dinner and looking after my younger brother and sister in the school holidays, until my mother came home at lunchtime from a part-time cleaning job. Eventually, we moved to the Far Cotton area in Northampton in 1974, when I was 13 years old.

By the time I was 14 years old, I had lived at six different addresses and attended five different schools, so very close friends were not really a large part of growing up. The focus was always more on fitting in, a chameleon of sorts.

,

Generally, we always lived hand to mouth, but at least the violence towards us all by my father had stopped. However, it has to be said going forward under the 'hand' of my mother and the unsmiling rule of her new long-term partner was a marginal improvement. I had always stuttered badly as a child and continued to do so into my early 30's.

I got through my childhood school years by keeping my head down with assistance from my love of art and athletics. Prior to the 'Comprehensive School' system, I was fortunate at the age of 13 years old to receive a free transfer from Spencer Secondary School for Boys to Northampton Grammar School for Boys. Although it has to be said, I was very much in over my head.

At this point I would like to recognise those brilliant teachers who invested their time and those employers who looked past a gibbering idiot with a speech impediment to afford me opportunities.

I would also like to call out Mr Parsonson of Vernon Terrace School for mimicking my stammer in front of the whole class. Getting a cheap laugh at the expense of a 9 year old pupil must have really boosted your self-esteem as a role model of society.

Also, fellow Northampton Grammar School pupil David Palmer-Jeffery, who on spotting my meal tickets for 'free school meals' had a thick red line through them said, "You're a bastard aren't you?". I ceased eating at school lunchtimes and threw each week's tickets away for the rest of my years in school. If ever there was going to be a self-made man, it was going to be David, with the help of privilege and Daddy's money of course.

Looking back, I can't say life was hard, it was just different, as I have nothing else to compare it to as a child.

18

From about 10 years old, I endured endless under the radar bouts of depression. As a quiet child with a stutter and therefore not a lot of coherent speech to say, it was easy to hide. Most of my memories around this time seem to revolve around homework and being crouched on the floor drawing and painting to opt out of my surrounding.

During this time, I had tried to end my life by attempted hanging on a pair of braces at aged 11 (hilarious looking back), two aspirin overdoses between 14 and 17 years old that left me in a 'fish bowl world' like state for days and cutting my wrists and arms at 19 years old. No one was aware of the first three instances.

I must admit coping with school performance expectations, combined with all those hormones and emotions, was extremely challenging at the time.

I finally settled down at the age of 24 years old with my wife and we now have three grown-up children and five grandchildren. I didn't know what sort of husband and father I would be, but I was able to draw on my past to know what I did not want to be.

I had always grown up with the ghosts of my past, but the onset of serious balance issues in 2011, resulting in several operations 2013-2014 and residual ongoing balance issues made life very stressful, eventually being a factor in my decision to retire early.

Around this time, I saw a television programme about Stephen Fry's mental health issues. This inspired me to start writing poetry to stop the negative dark thoughts spiralling in my mind. A computer file became my partner in rhyme, as we hid my darkest thoughts together. This was the first time I had written poetry, since I was in secondary school at about 12 years old.

Soon after I retired, my best friend ended his own life, which was devastating. This resulted in a lot of guilt around why I hadn't spotted the signs or been able to prevent it. It was now evident we were both hiding our darkest thoughts.

During all this time my youngest daughter had also become very dismissive every time I gave advice or offered an opinion on anything. This finally came to a head just before Christmas 2020, when I had reached a point that I was no longer willing to feel bullied and disrespected, so spoke out. As a result, she left the house and said we would never see our grandson again. The upset I had now caused and unforeseen consequences particularly to my wife, resulted in me leaving everything and just walking away. I was eventually found by the Police later the following day after sleeping on a bench overnight in the freezing rain. I must own up to my intention to fall asleep in the cold and never wake up. At least then my wife could see my grandson.

This was the point 'Northamptonshire Mind' came into my life. The Police took me to 'Mind' in Northampton, this was the first time I had actually talked to someone. There were a lot of emotional tears and I can't praise Bernie Print at 'Northamptonshire Mind' enough for her support. Not only then, but her ongoing support and contact since. My doctor subsequently prescribed Sertraline, which has stopped the extreme highs and lows of my emotions, and I have received counselling through 'Northamptonshire Mind' in 2021.

Currently, I still take Sertraline daily and actually feel in control of my emotions for the first time since I was a child, so I expect this to be ongoing. I have accepted that the medication addresses the chemical imbalance in my brain and restores more balance to my emotional well-being. I can't escape the past and I'm not sure anyone ever recovers from it. It's what has shaped me, so I have learnt to accept it and try to keep it in perspective.

Having very few secrets left to hide, I have shared many of the lighter poems with close friends and all the poems with a couple of volunteers at 'Northamptonshire Mind', who suggested I should publish them. Many of the poems towards the end of this anthology are a introspective look back at some of those past events.

I discovered poetry was a way of writing down my thoughts, to get them out of my head and stopping them spiralling around. It was also useful as a barometer to look back and know I was going to be okay, as there had been times I had felt worse. Throughout, it would appear I kept some humour in my darkest moments. Ironically, it would appear from my writings that my life is in reverse, with most of the adult issues being in my childhood and as I heal my mind returns to childlike observational humour.

This has been a very long journey and realised I had to deal with my own mental health issues, before I could contemplate being so open. I am hoping these poems may help others to realise no matter how dark things may seem, you are not the only one that feels this way and it can get better. Often the first step back from the abyss is traumatic, but just saying to someone 'I'm struggling to cope!'
is a huge step forward.

Table of Contents

Poker-Face - The ability to lie convincingly!

Nature At My Fingertips

Guardian Angel

The Swiss Army Utility Knife

Everyday People

Once Upon A Time In Northampton

The Mad Hatter

The Last Word

To The Keeper Of Secrets (*My PC*)

Thank you for helping me not feel so alone,
So please accept my humble offering of this personal rambling tome.
Of rhyming thoughts from in my head,
As writing keeps me from the dead,
Please do with them as you will,
I write whenever I've had life's fill.

I find it clarifies my mind,
To write my thoughts down in a rhyme.
And once I finally get them out,
It helps me banish mortal doubt.
This process of self-mocking thoughts,
Exposes all, including warts.

No excuse for this dark humour,
I'm excising my personal tumour.
I know I'm not quite right you see,
I'm in my head, the joke's on me.
I hope one day these thoughts will stop,
Perhaps I'll just get writer's block!

31

Embers

Sue blows on my ashes and the embers glow,
Where is my life going? I don`t really know!

Is this for good or is this for bad?
I`m loving the ups, but hating the sad!

I feel like a teddy that`s put to the side,
Tatty and battered, loose stuffing inside!

But not all toys are games for occasional play,
Put away and forgotten for some rainy day.

They need to be treasured, feel loved and adored,
Not kept in the dark, messed about and ignored.

I don`t like these feelings and wish that I could go,
Sue blows on my ashes and the embers glow.

Winter Warmer

Life is cold, when you get old,
As winter lingers longer.
At least I know, that when I go,
Below will be much warmer.

The Mask

I have these feelings deep inside,
The sort that we all try to hide.
Although they're not the sort to share,
They twist and stab, and hurt, and tear.
On the outside I'm John, I smile and I quip,
I don't take off my armour, it's such a cosy fit!
When left on my own, I just might shed a tear,
But if I don't let you in close, I have nothing to fear.

Sunday Afternoon Out With The Parents

Ever had one of those days,
Where blue skies turn into greys.
The wind blows cold and spits of rain,
Trees have no leaves and memories pain.
Winter birds don't sing, but mooch about,
A rising feeling of self-doubt.
Ever had one of those days,
Those childhood, cemetery visiting days.

Soul Hole

My heart has a hole,
It lacks a soul.
For what is a heart with a soul?
Whole!

55

55 and still alive,
By now I hoped I would have died!
This Catholic boy, born out of sin,
Whose mum was told to drink the gin.

I`ve had dark thoughts since I was ten,
Now they return to me again.
I never planned to get this far,
It looks like God has raised the bar!

Eyes Wide Open

I have an emptiness inside,
The sort that makes you think you`ve died.
It`s wormed its way inside my head,
Into my sleep, whilst I`m in bed.
It wills that God my soul should take,
Before the morning when I wake.
But when I open up my eyes,
To disappointment and surprise.
To my detriment and demise,
The world`s a tissue of little white lies!

The Companion

I know you`re always with me,
But never by my side.
You skulk inside the shadows,
As in the dark you hide.

You`re always just behind me,
When I turn out the living room light.
Your world it surrounds me,
When I close my eyes at night.

You must be very shy,
As you never show your face.
You always keep me company,
When you know, I need some space.

You must be very patient,
To wait around for me.
You must be Oh, so lonely,
How can I set you free?

I`m very pleased to meet you,
I think I know your name!
But think I shall not utter it,
As I think we are the same.

I recognise your awkwardness,
You always have to cover.
I recognise the thoughts inside,
The ones you try to smother.

So, come sit down beside me,
While we talk about the past.
We have all night to talk,
And it just might be my last.

We can talk about the good and bad,
And how I lost the fight.
Perhaps you could then hold my hand,
Whilst snuffing out the light!

Jigsaw Puzzle?

A piece of me has gone inside, it must have been misplaced,
To lose something so important is an absolute disgrace.
To let my head lose sight of it, was such a big mistake,
I would have shared it freely, but life just seems to take!

A Nursery Crhyme

Like Old Mother Hubbard, the cupboard is bare,
I can`t find the old me hiding anywhere.

Jack`s fallen again and is now tumbling down,
Not like an acrobat, more like a clown.

I`m sat in the corner, sucking my thumb,
A taste that is bitter and not like a plum.

Old King Cole has his head in a sack,
So, all he can see, is darkness and black.

So Little Boy Blue come blow your horn,
No more time for sadness, no more time to mourn.

Call all the King`s horses and all the King`s men,
To put my Humpty Dumpty's head back together again.

Unlike the Old Woman who lived in a shoe,
I`ve been here before, so know what to do.

I`ll pick myself up and march that long walk,
Just like one of the soldiers in the Grand Old Duke of York.

Sometimes!

Sometimes I feel happy,
Sometimes I feel sad.
Sometimes I feel so good inside,
Sometimes I feel so bad.
Sometimes I just don`t know how I feel and I don`t think that`s fair,
Sometimes it all gets just too much and then I just don`t care!

Sometimes I look forward,
Sometimes I look back.
Sometimes I`m optimistic,
Sometimes the world is black.
Sometimes the world is yellow, with a little tint of blue,
Sometimes I think "what`s life about?", I haven`t got a clue!

Sometimes in the future,
Sometimes in the past.
Sometimes those awkward questions,
Sometimes need to be asked.
Sometimes I know the answer, the reason for my quest,
Sometimes is never really here, the present is the test!

Great Expectations

I try to be the person, that others want me to be,
And sacrifice the dreams inside, so I cannot break free.
I'm rather like a Kinder Egg, with no surprise inside,
An illusion of my real self, before your very eyes.

Living my world inside my head, is not my favourite place,
Dark with old cold memories, disappointment and disgrace.
Once in a while, you just might see me in a glassy stare,
I've gone back somewhere in my head, so I'm not really there,

The world of expectation, is just too much to bear,
When all our lives are intertwined, a burden we all share.
Grief, heartache and sorrow, are the lake in which we drown,
Like removing blocks in Jenga, my thoughts keep tumbling down.

If I could guarantee the end of me would not leave a mark or stain,
I would gladly let go of everything and pour it down the drain.
I didn't choose this life and certainly not who I'm supposed to be,
So, take this husk, that's been my home and give away rent free.

God has no place inside my life, he left me years ago,
No inner peace or happiness, nor thoughts that make me glow.
So why do I continue within this miserable abyss?
The depressing thought the afterlife might just be worse than this!

Crabby Attitude

Don`t talk to me, don`t even look at me, cos I don`t want to know,
Don`t call or even ask me out, cos I don`t want to go.
Don`t write to me, knock on my door, keep a hundred miles away,
Leave me alone inside my shell, it`s where I want to stay.

I don`t want to hear your moaning, I don`t want to hear your voice,
This isn`t any other day, where I have no f***ing choice.
Keep the hell out of my life, I just don`t need the stress,
I`m not a bloody Pawn, in your game of people Chess.

Don`t bitch about me to others, so keep your big nose right out,
And if I feel the need to curse out loud, I`m going to scream and shout.
I`m done with all the politics and being so polite,
Leave me alone to stew a while up to my neck in shite.

In Recovery

Something burning in my chest, has given me a fright,
I peeped inside and to my surprise, I saw a pilot light.
Deep in the dark, I must have sparked,
But no one else noticed or remarked!

The Arrivals

Connie`s coming round to play,
Hip! Hip! Hip! Hooray!
Although she isn`t quite yet four,
She`ll soon be knocking on my door.
With curly hair and glowing smile,
Connie`s come to play awhile!

She`ll bring her sister Lottie Lou,
With a cheeky smile her eyes look through.
We`ll play some games and laugh, they`re clever,
Oh, how I wish they could stay forever!
Connie`s coming round to play,
With Lottie Lou, Hip! Hip! Hooray!

The Trick

I have a trick, that keeps me alive,
It gives me a purpose and the will to survive.

The trick is not mine, it`s nature`s of course,
And probably it`s most unstoppable force.

It`s not the people around me, whom life taints judgmental,
The very same ones that can send a sane head mental.

It`s the babies and small children, so new in my life,
That turn my head soundly from pills, noose and knife.

They give me the lift in my heart and my head,
So, I can sleep soundly, asleep in my bed.

They just want to be loved and give love in return,
Giving smiles, hugs and kisses, a lesson to learn.

No premeditated agenda, no tricks on your mind,
An honest relationship, that`s just so sublime.

So, when my head turns to the dark and I stray,
The thoughts of these children keep my ghosts at bay.

Just Sitting Around

Excuse me if I sit a while and watch the world pass by,
If I`m quiet, I`m invisible, just like a Secret Spy.
From here I gain perspective of just where I fit in,
Between the smoking shelter and the rubbish recycle bin.

Forgive me if I sit and smile at all that`s gone before,
As without a sense of humour, white coats will knock upon my door.
There`s such a lot to laugh about, but please don`t take offence,
If you could see inside my mind, you`d see I have no sense.

Pardon me if I sit and think of all that`s yet might come,
The future isn`t set right now, the battles not yet won.
If I can just get through today and face up to tomorrow,
Perhaps in a small humble way, I can save someone sorrow.

The Dreamer

Everywhere I go I always see the memories of my past,
It's written on each place in Indian ink, just like a permanent scar.

I wish that I could close my eyes and make them disappear,
But even in the darkness they remind me they're still here.

It's even in the things I do and the words that people say,
It's in the smell amidst the air and the weather of each day.

And if I had a magic cloth to wipe the whole world clean,
I could stop remembering and use the space to dream!

Pinch Me, To See If I`m Here!

Often it occurs to me that I`m not really here,
If that`s the case, then I could go with nothing left to fear.

Often, I think life`s beautiful, like softly falling snow,
Always nice to look at, but can`t wait for it to go.

What if my whole world is just a construct of my mind,
No future, past or present and no footprints left behind.

Chameleon

The world is full of colours that we wear upon our skin,
The brightness and the hue denote the mood that we are in.
It`s not hard to hide from the outside, the true colours within,
When despair, desire and frailty are hidden by a grin.

I look into the mirror, to see who I might see,
It`s no one that I recognise, it`s certainly not me.
I don`t recognise that frown or the stare from those dark eyes,
The down turn mouth, that long drawn face, like some cartoon disguise.

It`s not that jolly character I would like to be,
Shiny bright and colourful, like the brightest Autumn tree.
If I could slip out of this skin and see what`s coiled inside,
It would be black and wet and slippery and very serpent like.

Inside this world I`m awkward, I really don`t fit in,
So, I have to hide the child inside, behind the smiles and grin.
It really doesn`t matter which world, or the planet that I`m on,
I can blend in easily, as I`m a chameleon!

Wishing Well

I wish I could find it in myself to hate that very name,
The one that thinks that other lives are really just a game.
I wish I could find it in myself to turn the other cheek,
But if I`ve nothing good to say, no evil should I speak.

I wish I could find it in myself to hold my head up high,
Then I could feel so tall again and nearly touch the sky.
I wish I could find it in myself to laugh out loud and smile,
I might just then forget myself, perhaps once in a while!

Wandering Star

I`m out here in the distance and so very far away,
Above the clouds, I`m out in space, beyond the Milky Way.
You might just catch a glimpse of me, if you look in the night sky,
I`m the one that`s glimmering, just like a winking eye.
And if one day I find my guiding star back down to earth,
I hope to have my sparkle back and sense of own self-worth.

Colour Me In

When I`m sad my colours grey,
And reflective it is blue.
When happy I`m a sunny yellow,
When sick a greenie hue.
Sometimes I`m great, I`m in the pink,
And embarrassed when I`m red.
When things are going really well, I hit a purple patch,
And when I`m feeling quite morose, I`m really in the black.

When I`m in debt, I`m in the red,
In profit, in the black.
When I envy, I turn jealous green,
In shock, I look quite white.
Yet I can still be tickled pink,
And smell brown in a fright.
So where do all the colours go,
On dark nights when I`m feeling low?

Shipwrecked!

When the dark closes in and I stumble and I fall,
When my gaze is downward and I no longer walk tall.

When I feel like a plate that`s been smashed against the wall,
This is the time when depression comes to call.

Like woodworm damage below a galleon`s deck,
I`m a broken, abandoned and submerged shipwreck.

Incommunicado

"I meant to say, forgot to mention...."
Do I really have your full attention?
I know it`s so fantastically neat,
To email, text, Whatsapp and Tweet.
Or should I just revert to mime,
So not to interrupt Facetime.
I`m in the room, I`m here, it`s me,
It`s 'Mr Personality'.
Well that`s who I used to be,
Before the days of phone IT.

Complicated Relationship With Food

'Eggs over easy', that`s 'Sunnyside down',
`Funny face` ice lollies that are ate with a frown.
Spoon fed Trifle and custard by non-flying `Birds`,
And with `Alphabetti Spaghetti`, you can eat our own words.

A `serial` is something for breakfast we`re fed,
Steak Tartare is raw meat, like it`s never been bled.
When your `Goose is cooked`, you might hear it said,
'You`re toast', `Cream Crackered` or even `Brown Bread`.

Eating frogs-legs and snails, you`re not faring better,
As when eating French, it`s not usually a letter.
When eating a sprout, you leave no one in doubt,
You`re not keeping it in, but you`re letting it out.

`Sports Gems` allow us to eat out own hat,
While TV dinners advertise, salt, sugar and fat.
When swallowing Oysters do you wish you had flirted,
Does eating pudding alone, afterwards leave you `desserted`?

Do Champagne and Strawberries leave you aroused,
Whilst over indulging leaves you sleepy and drowsed?.
Does the sugar rush afterburn go to your head,
Do you secretly take biscuits back up to your bed?

What Am I?

I have silver skin to make me bright, I'm as wet as babies tears,
But I have no voice, I have no ears, so when speaking no one hears.

In sunlight's gaze I glisten, and I shine just like a mirror,
At nighttime I reflect the moon, I glimmer and I shimmer.

Water wings to soar about the deep, and tail to wag at leisure,
I share my world with creatures small, it really is a pleasure.

Alas, if I could be a bird, I would soar up in the sky,
To bid the Sun and Moon "Hello!" and touch the starry sky.

I would feed on fields of fine barley, wheat and corn and rye,
Then in a massive exclamation, I would give my voice try.

I would twitter and would chatter in code, to every other bird,
The joy that I could hear myself and also "yes" be heard.

Perhaps, I could be brightly coloured and flit among the trees,
Or hang around at bird tables and camera lenses tease.

Of course, this wish of mine is really quite absurd,
The reasons plain for all to see "I'm a fish and not a bird!"

That Feeling Inside (*Strangely non rhyming thoughts*)

Strange how a careless or intentional acerbic word can change my outlook
of the world.
From a blue sunny day, to passing through a transparent black veil.
Whilst adding weight and gravity to every single atom of my body.
Like sand in an egg timer, each atom trickles relentlessly from my head
like a life draining waterfall.
Momentarily pausing to pool in the bottom of my stomach, before again
moving downward.
Collecting in my heavy calves, ankles and feet before spilling over to add
to the dry sand dune my weary footsteps sink into as I labour uphill.
As my energy ebbs away, I slowly fill with melancholy.
Soon this moment will pass unobserved and fade away like warm breath
on a cold frosty morning.
Each time is never the same, just as every breath is unique in its own brief
existence.
This is merely another transitory moment in time, borrowed yet so
precious for the learning experience it brings.

Goodbye My Friend

You viewed the world through questioning eyes,
Narrated it with verbal surprise.
Those smiling eyes and sideways glance,
Telling truth from tall stories, we had little chance.
You liked to mix your words around,
And potter to tuneful humming sounds.
I'll miss the way you got bogged down,
The way you sometimes called me a clown.
I'll miss directions from the passenger seat,
Stopping off at 'Roadchef' for something to eat.
I'll miss our weekly full breakfast,
Our stomachs full and fit to bust.
I'll miss those endless mugs of tea,
Then queuing up to have a wee.
Generous and thoughtful my mate Al,
My closest friend, my biggest pal.
You always had an ear to lend,
So, thank you and goodbye my friend.
Hurry on board don't wait for us,
Departing now the last green bus.

*Written following the unexpected passing of my best friend, the most humorous
person I have ever met.*

61

Plotment Life!

We have plots of allotment on the Blisworth to Stoke Bruerne road,
With sheds, coops and greenhouses we share, with the occasional frog,
newt and toad.
We feed birds with seeds and fat-balls, that hang up on a tree,
The pheasants and mice feed down below, from the food that's dropped
for free.

We've organised our plots into wooden bounded beds,
We've weed suppressed and wooden chipped the paths, we must be
off our heads.
Added manure in the winter, when the allotment was in freeze,
We've dug the soil and have now to show our dirty gloves and knees.

The gully's filling nicely with unwanted weeds and veg,
Grass clipping, tree branches and occasional bit of hedge.
Bird families have nested snuggly in bird box, bush and tree,
Whilst Sue inspects and checks the vital signs of each hive Bee.

We have peas, beans and beetroot, all planted in straight rows,
We look like we know what we're doing, but only heaven knows.
The broccoli, kale and cauli's with their collars look so smart,
I'm looking at rhubarb, raspberries, strawberries and thinking of a crumble
or a tart.

We have seeds that grow much slower than the ever-present weeds,
We get nightly visits from animal wildlife and by day, passing bees.
We collect water from our rooftops, before it hits the floor,
Not enough days of rain so far, we really need much more.

With pheasants, mice and tiny birds it's a race to save our crop,
So, we cover them with tunnels, with pretty netting on the top.
We planted seed potatoes in the soil about 8 inches deep,
The rain has come, so now they pop their heads up from their sleep.

Occasionally on our days of toil, we'll stop and have a rest,
Choosing a seat that's comfortably and where the sun is best.
We'll eat our tasty sandwiches and drink from our coffee cup,
Whilst birds of prey fly overhead, so pigeons have to duck.

We'll carry on our merry day, till the plots are ploughed and scattered,
Then off to our homes for food and sleep, we really are quite shattered.
The birds would say, "you're winging it, you haven't got a clue!"
In our times of indecision, we think, "what would good old
Monty Don do?"

A Grand Day Out!

We're off on something, that's not quite a sport,
Not as fast as a march, but quicker than a walk.
Faster than a pensioner's rambler,
But slower than a young lamb's gambol.
Not sure whether you've been on one before,
We're off on 'Margaret's Magical Mystery Tour'.

Sensible footwear, sunscreen and caps,
With water laden rucksacks, upon sturdy backs.
Headed across the fields and up over the hills,
You'll need your asthma inhaler and prescription blood pressure pills.
She's leading us up the countryside path,
With her appointed Shepherd following aft.

Before leaving did you remember to use the loo,
As very soon it will be right out of view.
With very few bushes and no long thick grass,
Let's pray to God, we can hopefully last.
So should you decide to linger and wander,
They'll capture your blushes on digital camera.

There are lots of views and sights to see,
Patchwork vistas, with cotton wool trees.
Lakes and streams, reflecting the light,
Gigantic hills, in far distant sight.
And just as we get to the hilltops rise,
Into the vales, we gradually glide.

The sound and sights of differing birds,
Get 'twitching' soon, the bird spotting nerds.
They pick up so keenly, the distinctive bird sounds,
And use laser like eyesight whilst tracking them down.
A 'twitchers' day out is never complete,
Without an intriguingly rare, 'twitter' or 'tweet'.

Out in front, the seasoned veterans race,
Leaving novices, out of breath and off the pace.
The trek line grows like an elongated snake,
Whilst back markers stop and nice photographs take.
Just when the stragglers lose touch with the bunch,
We'll stop for a breather and camp down for lunch.

Sandwiches, sausage rolls and baguettes galore,
Pork pies, salads and oh so much more.
Chocolate bars, energy bars, cake and fruit,
Everyone opening rucksacks of culinary loot.
We hope, but not for granted we ever would take,
That Beth or Margaret, have both baked a cake.

After copious cups of tea, or drinks of cold water,
We're off again walking, like lambs to the slaughter.
Our lead filled legs don't seem to work so well,
And the blisters and tired calves are starting to swell.
And now that our tummies are full of heavy bounty,
So, I'm wishing I had a horse, just like a Mountie.

As our destination finally comes into sight,
We summon all our energy with all of our might.
To plod the final steps to our destined location,
The end of our journey and our trepidation.
We've all made new friends amongst the roving crowd,
And Margaret's guided us safely and done us all proud.

It's almost evening and still summer light,
We survived sore limbs and the odd insect bite.
So now we off t' brewery to go on a tour,
There's always great interest and room to learn more.
Then off t' pub, for ale, conversation and snap,
Before saying goodbye and late travelling back.

Exposure

Without clothes and personality, we would really feel exposed,
From the hair upon our heads to the nails upon our toes.

Our bodies like the universe, mole scattered just like stars,
It digests the food we eat and deposits it as Mars.

Knees and elbows like a tortoise, that get often rough and dry,
Legs that lift our bulk and carry it, to where we wish to lie.

Eyelids our shutters to the world and all that we would spy,
Protecting the lens our brains see through and hide us when we cry.

Our arms and hands combine to hug the people we let in,
The tiny bones inside our fingers fitting glove-like into skin.

Liver and kidneys deep inside, would make dinner at a price,
But when they're coming from our own bodies, then the thought is
not so nice.

We are all very different people from the top down to our toes,
And to comfort our personalities we decorate and cover up, with ink,
jewellery and nice clothes.

We take the time to frame our face and to titivate our hair,
Then we ask ourselves and wonder, why does everybody stare!

A Little Unclear

I am the man with the faraway Sertraline stare,
I'm not really here and I'm not really there.

Emotional feelings are no longer allowed,
I am the man whose head is a cloud.

I am the man who's curled up in a ball,
Cuddling himself tight, as asleep he does fall.

I am the man whose too long for his bed,
I am the man with the clouds in his head.

I am the man who stood tall and proud,
At least a foot above most, but most often head bowed.

I am the man with his head in the clouds,
I am the man whose head is a cloud.

The early days of taking Sertraline.

A Giant's Tale

At times the thoughts inside my head,
Leak out as words, best left unsaid.
So, to not offend or worry those around,
It's often best to write them down.
Like a garden watering can spout,
The memories kept on trickling out.
Whilst the watering can was overflowing,
The BFG just kept on going.
Push to the side and trodden down,
The troubled thoughts produced a mound.
Like a carbuncle on a bike,
The air released by a sharpened spike.
The pressure blew up in my face,
Exposing my privacy and personal space.
The Genie's out the bottle, the cat's out the bag,
The whole occurrence a big red flag.
The past and the present both collide,
Hold on tight for a bumpy ride.
The boil lanced, the wound exposed,
It seems like every man and his dog knows.
But strangely with the help I've had,
The mound's not a hill and not so bad.
I sat inside my living room,
Awaiting my 1:30pm weekly counselling Zoom.
To talk about the 'ups' and 'downs',
With Da-Sheena Fulford (she/her pronouns).
Putting old memories into a box,
Like a bedroom drawer full of holey socks.
Although the random thoughts sometimes raised doubt,
I feel much better now they're free and out.
I'm much more settled and in control,
Perhaps this time I'm on a roll?

Me And My Shadow (*A poem for Lucy my cat*)

Lying down or sat relaxed in a chair,
My tiny shadow`s always there.

From squeaky chirps just like a mouse,
To tractor purring that shakes the house.

Like potting plants into the ground,
Then clawing back and settling down.

My guardian angel, baby black bat,
Coils up asleep upon my lap.

Eggs Exit! (*Eggs uneasy and over!*)

After dropping out of a chicken's backside,
There really isn't anywhere to hide.
Nowhere to run, for new laid eggs,
Because they have no arms and legs.

You might think, they would just roll about,
Wobble a bit, or even shout!
But without eyes, where would they go?
Which direction, how would they ever know?

Without a mouth, they have no voice,
Which only leaves a simple choice.
So, make your mind up quickly and decide,
How do you like your eggs, scrambled, poached, boiled or fried?

Now poached is like having your skin removed or in this case the shell,
Then boiled in salted water, it's an egg's version of hell.
Boiled in the shell, trapped inside, is certainly not a joke,
To then have the top of your head chopped off and a soldier poke your
yoke.

Pan fried eggs are all laid out, exposed and lying on their side,
Then doused in oil, butter or fat, whilst gently fried alive.
Imagine being scrambled, mixing your body and your head,
Or trying to just hide away, in two slices of 'delicious' fresh crust bread.

The lucky ones are fertilised and left inside the nest,
To hatch out and grow up to be, a chicken like the rest.
A chicken's life looks easy, but it's less long lived for men,
As men are Cock's and therefore, not as valuable as Hens.

In days gone by, most Hens lived in a farmer's barn battery,
Free Range, they now can stretch their legs and run about with glee.
So, when eating Roast Chicken dinner, spare a thought for humble eggs,
From just below the Parson's nose and between those tasty drumstick legs!

*This poem was inspired by finding out, an Ostrich has eyeballs larger than the size
of its brain. Therefore, although the Ostrich may observe a lot, it is probably not
very bright! This poem is further evidence, together with my long legs and neck...
I may be an Ostrich!*

The Plot's Lost

The allotment isn't quite the same, when Gemma's not around,
The Sun stays low below the clouds, as if to wear a frown.
The summer plants are dying and the weeds have gone to sleep,
The Dahlias have lost the will, they bow their heads and weep.
The chickens have stopped laying and protest sat in their coup,
No more cold drinks upon the plot, it's hot coffee or soup.

There's hope Gemma will pop out soon, the early shoots I've seen,
It's in the Autumn garlic, onions, peas and the broad beans.
The Black Kale is still standing, like a line of small palm trees,
Winter cabbages are growing bigger now, almost up to our knees.
Brussels standing to attention, with their tunic buttons in a row,
With the Parsnips waving feather green flags, they're putting on a show.

Christmas is approaching, some holders have lost the plot,
This growing game continues in the cold and not just when it's hot.
Although in the winter the allotment can be a quiet and lonely place,
The grey and cold can always be banished by a friendly, cheery face.
For now, the allotment seems to have lost its energy,
But when the Sun in Gemma is on the plot, it's glorious to see!

*A token of appreciation and support for Gemma Roberts of Blisworth Allotment
Association, going through a difficult time.*

72

Locked Down

Locked down due to Covid and secure inside our homes,
We spend more time in the garden, where we potter just like gnomes.

We hide away from coughs and the places people touch,
To be asked to just self-isolate is really not too much.

Although the days we isolate continue to increase,
Spare a thought for those less fortunate, infected and deceased.

Meanwhile get those little jobs done, you didn't have time to do,
Check on friends, relatives and neighbours, to name but just a few.

And if you're tempted by the weather away from home to stray,
Remember to keep your distance and your Colgate breath away.

Don't get bogged down chasing toilet roll or hand sanitising gel,
Just wash with soap and water and gently waft away that smell.

Going Through A Change

I use to think that feelings and emotions were the same,
But I've had a bit of time to think, on where to lay the blame.
I still feel love, desire, have empathy, experience loneliness and pain,
I'm more calm, relaxed and comfortable, with the 'new' chemical
in my brain.

Emotionally dampened to the extremes of happy, angry and sad,
Life seems a whole lot easier and so, that really can't be bad.
Arousal is the link, I think, to emotional response,
Driving those thoughts to a level, where they lead a merry dance.

It's rather like a parasite, that feeds upon emotion,
Twisting those darker inner thoughts, in a downward spiral motion.
Sometimes I feel guilty, the emotion has now gone, to cry,
Where once the waterfall ran fast, it's now completely dry.

I would speak in terms of how I felt and not in how I thought,
In the trap of high emotions, like a hooked fish, I was caught.
I still worry about the future, whilst still looking at the past,
But more balanced thought processes mean, the dye has not been cast.

I thought my rambling rhyming writings would eventually just stop,
But it appears I still can feel things, just no emotional, big drop.
My mind still walks between the lines and stays within the range,
It's really just adjusting, as I'm going through the change.
It doesn't mean I don't think about important things and react to
the world around,
It just means I have my size 11 feet, planted firmer on the ground.
So, after a year on Sertraline, I've now been left to ponder,
Feelings are not the same as emotions, as they are the First Responder.

*Inspired by trying to understand the changes to my mental health
in the past year.*

74

The Angel Of The North

The `Angel of the North` came down, to stay in Thorpe Astley,
To bring sparkle to Leicester and the Everards Christmas Tree.
Although of late that spark was lost, except for a tiny glimmer,
It has started to shine bright again, to twinkle and to shimmer.
It's in the eyes, it's in the smile of this beautiful Geordie girl,
Just like the Christmas Fairy in a glittery ballgown Christmas twirl.
This Angel born is Newcastle, it's my honour to know,
As the spark and fire back inside of her, will only grow and grow.
We know that when we both need someone, we'll always have a friend,
To listen when we need it most and have an ear to lend.
With the Festive Season upon us, the Angel's time to see family,
To sit around the Christmas table and open presents from under the tree.
So, with daylight getting shorter in the winter waning sun,
It's a long drive towards those Northern Lights, by M1 and A1.
Christmas is time for family and not a time to be alone,
So, when she sees the Angel of the North, she'll know she's nearly home!
Have a wonderful Christmas Claire and fantastical New Year,
Have lots of food, have lots of gifts, but just not too much beer.
When the time comes to head back south, you just won't want to go,
So, make sure when you come back to us, that you bring the Mistletoe.
I look forward to meeting up again in 2022,
When the Angel of the North is shining and the sky is clear and blue.

Returning the support to my friend Claire Cannell, who deserves better than life returns to her. Always bubbly, the life and soul of the party on the outside. A fellow chameleon!

The Obsession Of Time

How can we focus on the now?
When scientists focus on the how!
When telescopes face to stars in the black,
How can we ever stop looking, both forward and back?

Time obsessed humans have never enough,
But we don't know how much we have, so that's pretty rough.
We stress that we've arrived too early and worry we'll be late,
As if time is something we control and not aligned with fate.

Time is elastic as it drags, or goes so very quick,
Like wading waist high in treacle, or sliding on an oil slick.
The sands of time, it ebbs and flows,
As the future shrinks, past history grows.

Hands marking time on life's face like a clock,
Record at second pace, with a ticking and a tock.
As the minutes and hours, go sailing by,
Years, days and weeks, seem like they fly.

Time is often too short, so we wish to turn it back,
It allows bad thoughts to fester or heal up life's tiny cracks.
The past can hold you back, which is the heavy weight of time,
Whilst the future transports us forward, our guide through s
pace and time.

When the present reaches our senses, it's already in the past,
As time is only relative and never meant to last.
'Time and space' is something different, when we need to slow things
down,
Sometimes quietly on your own, or just with those close around.

Sometimes we have too much on our hands, so we can share
, waste or relax,
We can have time to reconsider our actions, or just enjoy it to the max.
There's a time to be born, a time to live and when times up, a time to die,
A time to cherish, a time to fear and even laugh and cry.

From waking up time, to bedtime, through school or work and leisure,
We have breakfast, lunch, dinner and snacking times, when eating
is a pleasure.
Summer and Winter holiday times, are always worthy of a note,
These are the times to decompress, or whatever floats you boat.

Memories are so important, special by the fact they're chosen,
An attempt to go back to a point, where time it stopped and frozen.
Frozen in time memory has a little trick, when commanded to recall,
Those specific tiny details, are not quite so clear at all.

Perhaps the most important times, are those we choose to share,
That very act of choosing, means emotionally we care.
There's a time to wait, a time to stay and even a time to go,
So, stop clock-watching your life away and just go with the flow!

Modern Life

Mobile phones and tablets are an excellent distraction,
You can text your friend, who has just left, something you didn't mention.
An alternative reality, where we can get immersed,
Even the tiniest tots on keyboard skills, seem to be quite averse.
So many unusual topics and interesting things to see,
You can look up how to do things and download things, all for free.

There are people called influencers, who can persuade your buying power,
Sellers and food services, that can be delivered within the hour.
Bloggers wanting to sway the way you think, to their own thoughts and
views,
You can catch up with the world around, using WhatsApp, Facebook,
Twitter and the News.
Everything that's ever been in the world, inside your Living Room,
Even....................

Normal Service Will Be Resumed As Soon As Possible!

Sorry, someone just sent me a very, very, very important funny 'meme'.
Where was I now?
I've forgotten, I must have got distracted……. again!

Revisiting 'Incommunicado'.

Sue-Sue

Sue-Sue doesn't eat fish, or any type of meat,
But on her plates piles lots of lovely vegetables to eat.
Loves cheese, but only eats eggs when hidden in disguise,
Inside cakes and quiches, but not with drawn on mouth and eyes.
Likes salads, soups, rice, pizza and different shapes of pasta,
Has been a vegetarian since 17, I should know I've asked her!

Inspired by my grandson's name for my wife and the fact she is a vegetarian.

Fuel Poverty Blues

Hey there, have you heard the News!
The increase in fuel poverty blues.
Between heat and food, we'll have to choose,
Wear cardboard soles in holey shoes.

Whilst Superpowers posture war,
Young Oliver Twist's will want for more.
Low-income families can't afford a loan,
While hungry little tummies, gurgle and groan.

So, pile rugs and coats upon the bed,
And snuggle up to Little Ted.
As in the morning they'll be no heat,
Just icy white, numb cold feet.

Waking up to a frosty white surprise,
The window ice is now inside.
Upon the ice, children scratch their name,
Whilst anguished parents feel the shame.

To eat, or heat, or pay the rent?
It's like a never ending 'Lent'.
With debt that income just can't meet,
Evicted out on to the street.

Human duvets, in closed shop doors,
On urine scented, cold stone floors.
Invisible to those passers-by,
That look with a judging blinded eye.

Whilst policymakers promise more lies,
That severely impact on our daily lives.
Food Bank shelves run out of supplies,
As a mother and her cold, hungry infant cries!

Inspired by January 2022, energy and food prices. Whilst also reflecting upon my childhood.

The Bucket List Of Endless Improbable Possibilities

I want to…
Love and never feel heartache.
Be hugged like I hug my cat, by someone who really loves me.
Be held like I'm the most precious thing in the world.
I want them to never let go, so I feel small and safe.
Always feel deeply, but never experience its emotional pain.
Love someone and never feel guilt.
Never look back or forward and enjoy the moment.
Only affect the lives of others with their best interests at heart.
Always leave someone in a better place than I found them.
Always put myself in the other person's shoes, before I speak or act.
Not worry how I am perceived by others.
Take onboard personal criticism, without being offended.
Never let my self-conscious undermine my self-confidence.
Decide and never harm others or regret my decisions.
Concentrate on the what is, rather than the what if.
Be liked by others for me and not for who people think I am.
Help others, but not be taken advantage of.
Not worry about money issues, nor have the worry of having too much.
Be thought of fondly when I've gone.
Tell someone I love them without feeling embarrassed or awkward.
Walk regularly and confide in someone I love.
Only be selfish if my personal well-being is under threat.
Be kind when confronted with vulnerability or hostility.
Never let anyone down, even if it is to my own detriment.
Take responsibility for my actions.
Be realistic in my goals.
Be comfortable with uncomfortable silence.
Never be invisible or make others feel invisible.
Listen carefully and understand without the clutter of my own thoughts
getting in the way.

82

Trust my intuition to always try and give others the benefit of the doubt.
Have my personal space when I need it, yet never feel alone.
Be open and honest, but not let my vulnerabilities be used against me.
Never be without music in my life.
Laugh and smile with self-confidence.
Never lose the humour and perspective of the child I'll always have in my head.
Always be there for my friends.
Listen with my heart and feel with my head.
Never feel I'm intruding by asking someone if they are ok.
Look for the positives in the bad.
Be awesome!

For A Friend

How often have you just sat quietly, for at least an hour,
And watched the chubby Bumble Bees, that buzz from flower to flower.
Caught sight of pretty Butterflies, flitting from cauliflower to cabbage,
Watched Red Kites soaring in the air, without the extra baggage.

Listened to the sound of water, bubbling on a fast-running stream,
Whilst watching shiny fish reflect, the colours in sunbeams.
Closed your eyes and felt the cool breeze, blow gently upon your face,
Walked casually taking in your surroundings and felt a sense of grace.

Strolled along the beach and felt the sand between your toes,
Whilst letting the waves wash away, your deepest fears and woes.
Looked up into a windy blue, cloud scattered sky,
And watched fluffy white cloud horses, go quickly galloping by.

Sat up and watched the sky at night, through to the crack of dawn,
To celebrate the Sun coming up, as each brand-new day is born.
It's okay to take some time out and give yourself some space,
Life's journey is a marathon and not a fast sprint race.

I write this poem for you, my good and valued friend,
Who for me, has always had, a listening ear to lend.
I know you're at a point, where you're feeling tired and shattered,
Try to relax, as your health and well-being is all that really matters.

Now, I know you need a bit of time and also personal space,
To put the jigsaw puzzle pieces back into their specific place.
I just wanted to say sincerely and make it very clear,
If you ever need or want to talk, Sue and I are always here!

*Written for my friend Teresa Fuller who has been one of the many people that
supported me through my mental health crisis. I can never repay the help I have had,
but I can pay it forward.*

Daffs Or Just Daft?

"Good morning, pretty Daffodils,
I bid good day to you!"
"How nice of you to open up,
But my favourite colour's 'blue'!"

*Inspired by rediscovering Spike Milligan's children's verse and seeing
the daffodils flowering on the allotment.
Looking back now, I see his influence on my childhood in many of
my poems. This is my tribute to Spike!*

85

The Gambler

I don't bet apart from one line weekly, on the Euro-millions Lottery,
I don't smoke and I drink rarely, so not an addictive personality.
I've had my share of up and downs, but sometimes plain bad luck,
Often, I've felt so depressed and stayed stuck in a rut.

I'm hoping that the worst of times, is firmly in the past,
And the present 'more positive me', is really going to last.
I'm looking forward to the world out there and just what I might find,
I hope I can always approach it with a kind attitude and open mind.

I'm taking a chance and gambling, that I'm going to stay around,
Leaving behind those dark thoughts, now all roulette chips are down.
I've realised I'm stronger than I thought and that feels rather nice,
So, things appear to be worthy of, another 'throw of the dice'.

I'm banking on the hope I have enough money to last,
So, I'll have to watch it carefully and not spend it too fast.
I'm taking a risk and putting my trust in new people that I meet,
And no matter how hard a task may be, never admit defeat.

I'm putting 'all my eggs in one basket', 'all in' in Poker terms,
'Betting on the river', as the final card up turns.
I'm betting on each day to be, a positive experience,
Like listening to old favourite tunes and maybe have a dance.

I'm making a wager, to be more positive,
To try to make a difference, to my life and how I live.
I'm willing to take onboard criticism and always try to listen,
Taking away as positives and consider it life's lesson.

I'm relying on help and support of friends, if I should ever relapse,
And I'll be sure to ask if things get tough, or I struggle to relax.
I'm hoping to back 'the winner', but I would be happy with 'a place',
I've 'jumped another hurdle' and 'still running' into space.

It's 'a dead cert' things are better, but 'the odds' aren't firmly fixed,
So, it would appear, I've become a Gambler, so of course I'm an addict.
If this addiction is the prize and price, that I have to pay,
I'll gladly take it with both hands, every single day!

*Inspired by preparing the allotment for planting potatoes. Aware we could still have
a frost, but still planning to grow vegetables for the future.it occurred to me I was
like a Gambler. Although Gambler's have a lot of bad luck, they are always
optimistic and convinced they will win. Like depression, they experience the high
adrenaline rush and that sinking feeling, but both often in very quick succession. Yet
they always believe things will get better and their luck will change for the better.
There's a bit of a Gambler in us all, I think!
Or am I just swapping one addiction for another?*

Lesson For A Frog To Learn

A 'Frog Prince', who lived alone in Roade,
Went off to court, a Lady Toad.
He said "There really is no doubt,
You're the most hideous thing, I've seen about".
"You stomach and your eyes bulge out,
You smell like an old decaying trout".
"You have warts and lumps upon your back,
And any sense of urgency, you lack".
"You eat bugs and worms, with your sticky tongue,
Your digestive system, is just so, so wrong".
"Your feet are webbed, with toes and claw,
And you've a double chin, under your jaw".
"You have slimy lips and long wide grin,
And that nasty green colour, on your skin".
The Lady Toad replied curtly, "You're not much better looking than me,
And if you had got to know me first, there's more to me, than
you can see".
"I don't leap about judging and jumping to conclusions,
And I certainly do not subscribe, to your 'Royal' self-delusion".
"So off you hop, with some advice, I'll happily give for free,
As 'shallow' seems to be the depth, of your personality".
"It's better to be kind and consider the feelings of another,
And never judge a book, just by its unattractive cover!".

*Inspired by all the brave people out there, that are misjudged by
the first impressions of others.*

88

Percy The Garden Snail

Percy the Garden snail,
Has a limp and looks quite pale.
Eyeballs on stalks, that look so odd,
Because Percy is a 'Gastropod'.

Unlike a slug, that travels alone,
He has to carry around his home.
So, with this huge weight upon his back,
Percy doesn't waste time hurrying back.

He can camp down and rest, whenever he needs,
Hidden below the flowers and the weeds.
And at the end of his silver trail,
He can tuck in his eyes, his head and tail.

Percy doesn't always get relationships right,
But who cares, he's an 'Hermaphrodite'.
So, why does he limp and slide.? Just look!
Percy only has one foot.

89

Milli-Cent

Cyril the Centipede, it was said,
Kept odd shoes and socks under his bed.
Having lots of legs to walk about,
He would climb up trees and hang about.

His girlfriend, 'Mary Millipede',
Had lots of time, to roam and feed.
Cyril liked to take young Mary out,
Although with more legs, she'd wear him out.

They would go out on romantic walks, it really was quite a giggle,
As Cyril would struggle to keep up and need to get on a wiggle.
Wiping their feet on the doormat, would take almost an hour,
But not as long as taking off their shoes and socks, when the
smell would overpower.

Said Cyril, "Mary, marry me?"
"We'll build our house, in a fallen tree!"
Said Mary, "Yes, I certainly will, I hope there's lots of rooms to fill!"
"I want to raise a family and really would like up to three!"

Cyril agreed to Mary's request and swept her off her feet,
Not an easy task at first, and it took time to complete.
When he held her in his arms, he looked lovingly into her eyes,
Then said "Shall we go and celebrate, with a burger and French fries?"

Mary's Hen Night was a grand affair, with all her tiny creature friends,
Wanda Wood Louse, Alice Ant and Edna Earwig would attend.
Whilst Cyril with his Stag Beetle mates, went out on a bash,
Ending up completely legless and sleeping overnight in trash.

They were married by Michael Maggot, inside his rotting apple church,
Just before Barry Blackbird spotted Michael, from upon his lofty perch.
Alas, poor Michael has left his church, so no more hide and seek,
Because it's plain for all to see, he's stuffed in Barry's beak.

Before Barry could spot them, they quickly wriggled away,
To live and love each other, for at least another day.
They trampled off blissfully, to raise a tiny family,
Inside the last remnants of, a decaying old oak tree.

After many weeks of expectancy, a baby girl was born,
Sometime between 3:30 am and the early light of dawn.
Cyril said "What shall we call our baby girl, she means so much to me",
Replied Mary, "Let's call her 'Milli-Cent' as she's half of you and me!"

Cyril said to Mary, "I think it's really neat",
"To hear the tiny pattering, of tiny little feet".
Mary said "Yes, it's very sweet and it certainly makes me happy",
"Unlike trying to get all those legs into, the longest baby nappy"
.

Terence Chapman

Terence Chapman is very old and wise,
And has tiny beady, slitty eyes.
Webbed feet and claws upon his toes,
And tiny nostrils on his nose.
He has very, very scaly skin,
But the oddest thing is 'the tin' he's in!

He always stays inside his shell,
And as he grows, it grows as well.
Like a deep-dish pie, that's upside down, he sunbathes and he stomps
around.
Looking for a juicy leaf,
Because he is the 'Dandelion thief'.

He sticks his head and long neck out,
And looks up, almost as if to shout.
If only, he had a voice to say,
It would probably be "have a good day!"
The joy this little fellow has brought us,
And how to 'chill out', Terence has 'taught us!'

*Inspired by my daughter Gemma's family Tortoise. Whilst also recognising my
thoughts have gone from thinking about self, towards noticing and thinking
about what's going on around me.*

You Are The Love Of My Life

I've taken you for granted of late,
Please back off, before I suffocate.
Although, I need a bit of space,
For you, I'll always have a place.
Not enough of you, it's fair to say,
Would absolutely, take my breath away.
I would certainly be 'blue',
If I didn't get enough of you.
Too much of you, can be corrosive,
And exposes your nature, volatile and explosive.
You always keep me 'in the pink',
Which has made me really think.
Without you, I would be retiring,
You're the difference between, expire and respiring.
You keep me safe, when fast asleep,
And when I have to dive down deep.
I hold my breath and count to ten,
As you my love, are 'Oxygen'.
'Oh! Oh!' or 'O₁ Two!
I just can't live, without you!

Inspired by initially thinking about the elements water, air and fire.
What transpired is more like a love poem for my wife.

93

Some People Look At The World Differently!

"Little Jenny's", had an 'op' on her little eye,
To let tears flow freely, till her ducts are dry.
"Has she got a big eye?", I hear you ask,
Yes! Jenny keeps it under a magnifying glass.

Life must be strange with two different size eyes,
One like a mole, the other like a fly's.
Through one, the world must look squat and small,
Through the other, big and fat, and tall.

Playing "I spy" must be so strange,
One eye too close, the other out of range.
But let's not be without a doubt,
Jenny would make a good, 'Crow's Nest' look out!

So, keep one eye open for "Little Jen",
Before she bumps into you again.
You just might find to your surprise,
She really has two normal eyes!

Inspired by my friend Jenny New having a "Little Eye Op".

The Scary Dare!

Schoolchildren always like a dare,
To challenge themselves, frighten and scare.
But the dare at 6, I would always hate,
Was at night through, Holy Sepulchre gate.
This shortcut from Sheep Street to Church Lane,
In daylight, just was not the same.
At night-time, cutting through in the dark,
My imagination, it would spark.

The thought, of all those buried bones,
Of the names upon, spooky headstones.
Gravestones like offset dragon's teeth,
Might hide a ghost, murderer or thief.
So, as my heartbeat loudly in my chest,
Quickened my pace, no place to rest.
Then, almost as I reach the street,
"BAH!" Sounds out loudly from a sheep.

Remembering just how scary it was as a child cutting through
the churchyard at night.

The Child In Me

I'm jumping into muddy puddles, to release the child in me,
I'm blowing pretty bubbles, that drift up towards the trees.
I'm looking at the world around and doing as I please,
I'm sorting out the things I know, from all life's mysteries.

I'm looking through my child's eyes, to find a sense of fun,
I'm collecting lots of lolly sticks, finding them one by one.
I'm playing with the tar on the road, that's melted by the sun,
I'm back in the school playground, where with friends I want to run.

I'm making the most of summer holidays and going to the park,
I'm playing out on long sunny days and going to bed before it's dark.
I'm going on a day trip holiday, by a dusty train upon a track,
I'm making sandcastles and paddling in the sea, as the waves roll
forth and back.

I'm learning to swim and stand firmly, upon my own two feet,
I'm now doing sums, I read and write, but not yet very neat.
I'm singing along with the radio, not in tune or to the beat,
I'm discovering the things I like and those I do not like to eat.

I'm playing 'cowboys and Indians', I'm playing 'tag' and 'fleas',
I'm playing football in the street, tearing my trouser knees.
I'm getting up to mischief and climbing high in trees,
That's why my mind's jumping into muddy puddles, reminding
me of me!

Inspired by the lovely Easter Holiday weather and looking back. Completes
my life so far, as a circle in many ways.

96

Gibberish

The little boy inside my head,
Still stammers and still wets the bed.
Stands up in class to read aloud,
Amongst the childhood baying crowd.
The sniggers and incessant grins,
Keeps words deep down and stuck within.
With nought to say, but incoherent speech,
The thoughts inside his head he'll keep.
So best he stays inside my head,
Trembling in his wet pee bed.

Cadbury's Smash Instant Mash Potato (*For Mash Get Bashed!*)

My favourite food, if I must say so,
Is the wonderfully amazing, mashed potato.
I've loved it, ever since I was very small,
It could be the reason that I am so tall.
But 'Cadbury's Smash' potato, certainly was not,
It's disgusting when it's cold and not hot.
Eat the worst first, then the best is to come,
Was always the advice of my mum.
So, as a child of seven years old,
I tried to do, as I was told.
So, I left my 'Smash' to eat until last,
It then got cold and left me aghast.
It was horrible, so much it made me wretch,
I just couldn't eat it, not even at a stretch.
So, a good hiding and sent off to bed,
To think about, what I had been fed.
When allowed downstairs, put in front of me,
The same cold 'Cadbury's Smash', for my tea.
So, a further good hiding and to bed,
It was really messing with my head.
To my great displeasure and dismay,
Serve cold for breakfast and lunch, the following day.
Each time a good hiding and off to bed,
But I was quite stubborn, it must be said.
Then, finally on day two, for tea,
A new hot meal in front of me!

This was probably the first time I can remember feeling the indignation of feeling mistreated and being stubborn. I would have been about 7 years old, as we were living on 'The Mounts' in Northampton Town Centre at the time.

Sibling Rivalry

The 'Alpha Male' returns to rule,
My big brother is now home from his school.
In many ways, he's out to lunch,
So, I've become his boxing bag to punch.
I hope he won't be home for long,
He's just arrived, I wish him gone.

Recalling how the return of my elder half-brother in the school holidays was an opportunity for him to hit out, without being hit back at. A difficult time for him too!

Poker-Face - The Ability To Lie Convincingly!

At 13 years old, I was a newspaper boy,
To have pocket money at that age, was such a joy.
But a bully, on my paper round's estate,
Was about to take a hand into my fate.
To give up the job, I did decide,
Didn't tell my mother, so I lied.
But when my mother and her partner found out,
Their anger was far more than just to SHOUT.
And as I cowered on the kitchen floor,
In the corner betwixt the fridge and closed back door.
The blows came repeatedly, reigning down,
A steel poker, firmly held, in a 'brave' man's hand.
The lesson learnt, the purpose served,
No more than any liar deserves.
Ashamed and embarrassed, by my branded aching thighs,
I concocted an alibi, to deflect and to disguise.
And when asked at school to do P.E,
For weeks I would say "No Sir, not me".
"Can't you see, I've forgot to bring my P.E kit",
And "I've pulled my leg muscle, so it hurts a bit".
So, piling one lie upon another lie,
For two to three weeks, I muddled by.
The black lines of bruising are in the distant past,
But the scars run deep and will always last.

Recalling an experience of becoming a teenager and recognising that an unintended series of events had consequences, whilst my shame hid the real crime in plain sight. Interesting to note that throughout the rest of my teenage years whilst living at home, the atmosphere would change and my personality would diminish, whenever my mother's partner was in the room.

Nature At My Fingertips

Fly away Peter, fly away Paul,
My view from the playground, St. George's Infant School.
In the cold weather on chimney tops, the birds sit, twitter and chat,
As two fly away and to order, fly back.

Remembering my first year at school. The teacher took us into the playground to watch the birds on the chimney tops in winter. The birds really did seem to follow the words of "Fly away Peter, fly away Paul. Come back Peter, come back Paul". We even learnt the actions of holding up our index fingers on each hand and hiding them and unfolding them as we recited the rhyme. This to me seemed very magical at 4 years old.

Guardian Angel

I have never forgotten you,
I have felt you close by, at the most difficult times in my life.
Each turn and twist, you have been there to hold my hand,
You protected me and always tried to keep me safe.
Memories of us going to church together, sitting upstairs at the back,
How proud you were at my first Holy Communion.
How you once collect me from playing in the street gutter,
Applying a spit wash with a handkerchief, before taking me to a wedding.
You left suddenly, to become my Guardian Angel when I was seven,
But I never got to say goodbye, so in my memory you never really left.
Each and every decision I have made, you have guided me along the path,
I take full responsibility for my failings and credit you with my successes.
You shaped me as a little boy,
Even now as a 60 plus little boy, I still miss you!

*Touching my deepest emotional memory that has never gone away and
acknowledging the influence on my life of Jean (Jane Elizabeth) Eichmann
(nee Delaney) the wife of my father.*

The Swiss Army Utility Knife

This week I made a lovely new friend,
To her talents, there really is no end.
Compassionate, caring, bouncing with joy,
Surprising you like a 'Jack in the box' toy.
A singing voice that certainly gets my vote,
And fingertips that can strike a perfect note.
Her enigmatic personality,
Out there on show, for all to see.
If you meet her, it will fit into place,
When you see Lucy's wonderfully expressive face.
The sort of friend you hope you'll have for life,
Like a favoured Swiss Army utility knife.

Written for Lucy 'Tiggi' Neal of Northamptonshire Mind.

Everyday People

Just off Northampton's Regent Square,
A century's old path is trodden there.
Everyday people, some choose to ignore,
Queue patiently, outside the recessed door.

Above the Broad Street traffic din,
The sound of footsteps, welcomed in.
And as the numbers pick up pace,
The atmosphere makes the senses race.

To chat, to laugh, forget and play,
Or just to wile away the day.
Anxiety and emotional scars,
Forgotten for a couple of hours.

A smile upon life's hard worn face,
Feeling safe, inside this special place.
The signs are there for all to see,
The trust in you, the trust in me.

Circumstances to make a warm heart sink,
Comforted by a nice warm drink.
"Was that, no milk added in your tea,
Or white, two sugars in coffee?"

Stories that inside, shed a tear,
Something you see, something you hear.
It makes you question, how and why?
Think, but for God's Grace, there go I!

No sympathy, do the gathering ask,
But hope the smiles and laughs might last.
Coveting the comfort of their friends,
Until the transient session ends.

And when the time has come to leave,
They've had at least a space to breathe.
So, don't choose to simply walk on past,
Have the presence of mind, question and ask.

*For some everyday people that struggle just to get through the day, something
to look forward to is a very precious gift. The staff, students and fellow
volunteers at Northamptonshire Mind make that gift a reality.*

Once Upon A Time In Northampton

Old Northampton, once stood proud,
It was busy, vibrant, prosperous and loud.
Invested years in boots and shoes,
Pickering Phipps and Watney's, brewing booze.
Gibraltar Barracks inspected, regimented ranks,
Avon Cosmetics manufactured, on the Nene's banks.
Children bathed away the sun-filled hours,
Opposite Midsummer Meadow's cooling towers.
The 'Pavillion' thrived, on the Racecourse,
Where once jockey's raced, upon a fast horse.
The Emporium stood proudly centre, on The Parade,
With Church's China wares, set out and displayed.
Woolworths, Brierleys, Adnitts, Marks and Co-op,
Bustling tailors, banks and butcher's shops.
Littlewoods for fruit jelly and a cup of hot tea,
Mac Fisheries, opposite James's in 'The Drapery'.
Boots the Chemist adorned the corner of Gold Street,
Whilst the Market Square cobbles clattered, under leather soled feet.
Over 200 bustling and prosperous market stalls,
Selling everything from flowers, to hardware and tools.
The Fish Market sold, plump sea fish with big fat lips,
Whilst 'The Newlands' had long queues, for Friday fish and chips.
The Temperance and Bingo Hall, filled to the rafters,
School children queued eagerly at dinnertimes, for helpings of afters.
Cinema's, Odeon and the ABC,
Filled seats at almost every weekend matinee.
Public House's buzzed, as their piano notes rang,
With the sound of "My old man, said follow the van!"
Famous comedians took, the 'New Theatre's' mike,
Beat Policemen, walking or riding pushbikes.
Red Telephone boxes with thick Phonebooks,
Where queues wait their turn patiently, with long dirty looks.

Red and Green bus services, transport working class,
But Northampton's social prosperity was not meant to last.
Today, the town looks so dull and drab,
Slow days for the rows, of parked Hackney cab.
House prices now reflect this competitive age,
Unaffordable on, the average working wage.
Coffee shops sell cups of coffee, almost on a par,
With the cost of granules, purchased by the jar.
Fast food outlets jockeying, for space and first place,
Whilst fish and chip prices increase at fast pace.
Whilst industrial Northampton has now all but moved on,
Warehousing and University, now sing its new song.
The council now races to provide many more flats,
To cage prospective occupants, just like lab rats.
The signs of old Northampton, have now all but gone,
As the shops permanently close and footfall walks on.
Perhaps this old 'Shoe Town' has lost its heart and 'sole',
Maybe I'm looking fondly back, or maybe I'm just old!

*Inspired by reading the Spring Boroughs in Northampton's Town Centre was
purported to have been named so, because it was said that "so many villains
and criminals lived there, like rats in burrows".*
*The Spring Boroughs is currently under redevelopment, but to date the old
housing has been replaced predominantly by blocks of flats. Stacked cages with
no gardens, modern day society prison cells and the breeding ground for despair.*

The Mad Hatter

Never easy with letting people in,
Or cosy in my fragile skin.

Full of uncertainty, fear and doubt,
To others noisy and confident, from the inside out.

I now have a sense of inner peace,
High tide has calmed and waves decrease.

I might not be everyone's cup of tea,
But at least I am comfortable with me.

The Last Word

When the serious world of adults,
All gets a bit too much.
Remember to indulge the child inside,
As none of us grow up!

Ramblings and Rhymes of a Despicable Mind

*…(Breaking a few eggs
to make an omelette!)*

Part 2

Ramblings and Rhymes of a Despicable Mind...

...(Breaking a few eggs to make an omelette!)

Recognising anti-depressants bring a less erratic emotional balance to his life, John continues to write poetry and also his rambling thoughts in his own individual style, in an effort to come to terms with his past and present. John tries to explain the processes and reasoning behind his own thoughts and observations of the world around him. Only to realise how irrational, illogical and random they can be.

In excess of 95% of John's poems and ramblings are waking thoughts, formulated in rhyme and structured in his mind before getting up to write them down. This may be an indicator John's mind is rarely inactive and constantly processes his thoughts, even during sleep. This may give clues to his past negative downward spiralling traits, before chemically enhanced emotional control.

Dedication

This anthology is dedicated
to
my grandchildren.

I hope they never lose that childhood imagination and inquisitiveness
on their personal journeys, so thar they may answer for themselves
"Who in the world am I?"
as they grow into and discover who they are.

Acknowledgements.

Thank you to…
Those of you who have inspired many of these poems, listened,
supported and encouraged this second anthology.
My daughter Gemma for proofreading my work
and correcting my grammar.
My son Ross for formatting the cover design.

Ramblings and Rhymes of a Despicable Mind

...(Breaking a few eggs to make an omelette!)

A second collection of poems and ramblings continuing on a personal mental health journey

Foreword.

Originally, I set out with the intention to write a children's poetry book, but my obsession in the form of journaling in verse took over.

A much less shady anthology than 'Rambling Rhymes Through Difficult Times…', confirming my personal thoughts that there are no magic cures for mental health issues, just ongoing coping strategies.

I thought it important to record my thoughts as both poems and also ramblings in the order they surfaced, to highlight the randomness and difficulty in controlling them.

The first forty poems were written whilst at Northamptonshire Mind as a volunteer. Although brief, a privilege and life changing experience in so many ways.

Many of the poems are my way of thanking or supporting friends and my waking thoughts or questions.

So, from here the choice is yours, do you take the 'red' or 'blue' pill?

Table of Contents

The Moon

My Cat

Grant`s Coffee

Once In A While

Thank You For Coming

Floating Gently

Downtown

The Voice

Tiny

Those Blooming Birds

Relapsing

If You Can't Stand The Heat

An Indecisive Person

Rotherham Roger

The Favourite Shirt

Control

Twilight

I Have Questions!

Orthoworld

Paranoia

Brace

I Should Have Gone To Specsavers

Camera Shy!

Giving The Space To Stretch Our Wings

Tolerated

Mandy's Striking Matches

The New Religion

Ying And Yang

Opia

Throwing Away My Library Card

Mandy Sprinkles

I Camera

Look Out For Those Potholes!

Visually Paired

The Eden Project

Ebeneezer

Enabling Abel

Dotty

Lady Caterpillar

Out To Lunch, Arranging The Deranged,
Whilst Having My Ticket Punched

Night Watchman

Queue With A View

The Tea Party

Driver's In The Storm

Not Your Average Psychopath

Superhero

Hide And Seek

Some People

I'll Send In The Clown

Adventures Of The Real Baron Munchausen

Hairy Eyeballs

Grudgingly Nudged

It's Snow-time

Tooth Fairies

Common Sense

Letter To Lewis

131

The Moon

The Moon and I are intertwined,
A state of body, state of mind.
Like the moon controls the ocean tide,
It takes me with it for a ride.
So, before the sun comes up too soon,
Let's all go howling at the moon!

My Cat

Crouching down upon all fours,
With sharpened talons on it`s paws.
The cat, the master of the house,
Spots an unsuspecting tiny mouse.
With a shuffle and wiggle of backside,
The cat pretends to stop and hide.
Then with all his energy, every ounce,
Leaps up in the air with a mighty pounce.
But like a clumsy steeplechase horse,
He's completely missed the mouse of course!

Grant`s Coffee

Grant needs 20p,
The change for his cup of hot coffee.
He only has just 50 pence,
So 30p's a big expense.

Once In A While

Once in a while,
People often make me smile.
Sometimes when they make mistakes,
Or when they get the lucky breaks.
The bouncy dog with wagging tail,
The gentle singing of a whale.
An upside-down cat, stretching out,
Like rolling pastry or dough out.
A cheeky Robin, tilting its head,
Puffing out its red bib.
A baby fast asleep all warm,
Classroom mischief, going to form.
When you see me quiet, but with a smile,
It might just be one of those times, once in a while.

Thank You For Coming

Thank you, to those that came today,
I know some of you have come quite away.
I hope you got to write a rhyme,
Before we had to call it time.
I hope the words formed in your head,
Rolled out of pen or pencil lead.
On to paper creating art,
Head, pen and paper playing their part.
If more exploration you might seek,
I hope I'll see you all next week!

Floating Gently

Floating gently, as I glide,
Into a space, I no longer hide.
Sometimes there is no better space,
As all my thoughts move into place.
Leaving room to feel at ease,
And feel upon my face the breeze.

Downtown

I reflect upon the world around,
Each time that I go into town.
The smells, the sights, the very sound,
Of hustle and bustle, all around.
Burgers, coffee, fresh baked bread,
Up my nostrils, to my head.
Colourful people walking by,
Tall buildings almost touch the sky.
Such a wondrous, busy sight,
But, so much more threatening, dark at night.

The Voice

I have a voice inside my head,
It haunts me when I go to bed.
It whispers quietly in my brain,
It keeps me safe, it keeps me sane.
And when it's time for me to wake,
It's still in there, for heaven's sake!

Tiny

Taking tiny baby steps,
With tiny baby toes.
Heading in a direction,
Only a tiny baby knows.
Tiny baby fingers,
On outstretched tiny hands.
Touching tiny heart strings,
Like tiny rubber bands.

Those Blooming Birds

Have you heard those twittering birds,
Musically talented, beak-faced nerds.
Their songs, a mix of whistling bits,
It really does get on my…..nerves!

Relapsing

Sometimes I feel I'm falling, into the great abyss,
A darker place you'll never see and not as bright as this.
Threats at each dark corner, that try to pull me down,
A world of animosity, that tries to make me drown.
So, I often put pen to paper and put on my serious frown,
And try to think more clearly and write the dark thoughts down.

If You Can't Stand The Heat

I can't stand the heat,
From the top of my head, down to my feet.
It always makes me profusely sweat,
Like a horse being gelded at the vet.
I may be in my menopause,
Or at least they say, that may be a cause.

I try to stay cool in the shade,
And eat ice lollies, Lyons Maid.
It's no good looking cool and swelt,
If all you ever do is melt.
Perhaps I'll be okay in an hour,
When I've had a nice cold shower.

An Indecisive Person

An indecisive person called Grant,
Would pretend when he could, that he can't.
So, when it came to a break,
His own coffee he'd make.
And he'd even make one for his aunt.

Rotherham Roger

A rabbit in Rotherham called Roger,
Decided to take in a lodger.
So, he took in a hare,
And to his despair.
He had DIY skills like a Bodger.

The Favourite Shirt

I have a favourite shirt,
But to wear it, it would hurt.
For it does not fit anymore,
As my waist has grown much more.
It's rather tight around the arms,
But still has all its past memory charms.
It exposes my fat bulging belly,
As I relax and watch the telly.
So, it remains inside the drawer,
As age closes another door.

Control

How do I know I have free will,
When the world sees me as mentally ill.
Although sometimes the thoughts I think,
Make me low, makes me sink.
But when I'm really on a high,
The darkest thoughts they pass me by.
So, when my mind is on a roll,
The other me is in control.

Music

I have a tune inside my head,
It's been there since I rose from bed.
I can't even remember the tune's name,
But it sounds familiar all the same.
I can't remember who it's by,
No matter just how hard I try.
So, it plays on repeat for hours on end,
It's going to drive me round the bend.

Discography

45, LP or 78,
To get into music's not too late.
Whether Disco, Soul or Funk believer,
It`s not too late to catch the fever.
If you like mainstream, that's OK too,
Whatever moves and excites you.
And if it's Heavy Metal, or Rock'n'Roll,
It's not too late to lose your soul!

It's All A Matter Of Perspective

The world must seem big to an ant,
When climbing up a nice tall plant.
To get a better closer view,
Of what is what and who is who.
But ants have hopes and big, big dreams,
That's why they always work in teams.
No task too big, no task too small,
For a team of ants that are on the ball.
And as there is no 'I' in teams,
They help each other with their dreams!

Cat & Mouse

I love my cat,
He's white and black.
He`s long furred and fat,
And he's okay with that.
But if I was a creature, I would be a mouse,
And hide in the corner of a nice warm house.
At night I would roam and do as I please.
Whilst checking cupboards and fridges for tasty cheese.

Anger

Anger eats away at your heart,
Annoyance usually the start.
I try to keep anger in check,
But part of me thinks, "what the heck?"

Sometimes my heads in overload,
Full of things, fit to explode.
But once out, the flood starts to recede,
No angry left for thoughts to feed.

Change

If I could change the way I think,
And pour the old me down the sink.
I could make a start anew,
Look around enjoy the view.
I would take each new day as it comes,
And handle things with up turned thumbs.
So, if I want to really rearrange,
I alone can make the change.

Every Day's A Birthday

Sandwiches, pop, cake and jelly,
Fill me up and swell my belly.
Opened presents all around,
Whilst excited children leap and bound.

'Pass the Parcel', 'Musical Chairs',
'Hide and Seek' under the stairs.
"Thank you, for coming here to play,
But I lied….my birthday's still 3 months away!"

Ice Scream

Ice Cream,
Is why I scream.
That hot poker pain behind the eye,
That makes you want to pop it out or cry.
That intense pain on a sensitive tooth,
That makes you want to hit the roof.
Strawberry, raspberry, cherry, vanilla,
Cookie-dough, the real thriller.
Sweets, sprinkles and that sticky chocolate syrup stuff,
I feel so full, I've had enough.

Friends

Friends are like little gems,
Adoring the world around.
They show concern and check-in on you,
Whenever you are down.

Friends and not acquaintances,
Will never pass you by.
Friends will always sense your mood,
Stop you and question why?

Friends are always around,
When everyone else has gone.
Friends are the ones who cheer you up,
With laughter, fun and song.

Friends are loyal and long lasting,
Even when departed.
So, friends should never ever be,
Just taken for granted.

Freedom

Freedom to think within the norm,
Freedom to act within the law.
Freedom to speak, but not offend,
Freedom to hear and opinions lend.
Freedom to be and to exist,
Freedom to do a very long list.
But don't think I'm a naive fool,
I know I must stay within the rules.
I'm free to do whatever I wish,
So long as I conform…ish!

A Dulcet Rhyme

I know exactly where I fit in,
I'm the domestic garbage rubbish bin.
Why do I feel so out of place,
Not comfortable in my personal space.
Why does God not look down on me,
Does he not like what he might see.
Does he not like my dulcet rhymes,
Or does he just not have the time.

Flutterby

Sometimes I wish I was a butterfly,
Flitting freely in the sky.
Spotting cabbages to lay eggs,
Landing gently on my spindly legs.

Collecting nectar on my long thin tongue,
Coiled up, then outstretched and unstrung.
There really is no sweeter taste,
No better place, no better space.

Caterpillar children eating veg,
Climbing a tree, a wall, a ledge.
Alas, if I was a butterfly,
I would only have days to flutter by.

Beware The Happiness Thief

Did I smile too much today?
Did my smile not go away?
Did you see my shiny teeth,
Hiding from the happiness thief?
The type of thief who steals hope,
Makes life hard, to think and cope.
Those sharpened claws and sharpened teeth,
Dragging you down, way down beneath.
So, if you see my huge fat grin,
And wonder what kind of state, I'm really in.
Well with happiness and hope I know,
The happiness thief has nowhere to go!

Vulnerable

Curled and wrapped up in a ball,
In the corner, by the wall.
I just don't feel safe at all,
I am feeling vulnerable.

To the outside world I may look weak,
Should they care to take-a-peek.
Or even dare to try to speak.
To the stuttering, blubbering, big, tall freak.

Silence Revisited

Silence is a never-ending sound,
It permeates the world around.
It resonates in lamp-lit streets,
The running water in a creak.
The rustle of a leafy breeze,
The eerie silence of winter's freeze.
The constant dripping of a tap,
Snoring and breathing of a nap.
That self-talk in your head, you never mention,
Now has silence got your full attention?

Twinkle, Twinkle Little Rat

Twinkle, twinkle little rat,
Why do you sit and eat like that?
When you have four legs and not just two,
Is it so, you can admire the view?
When we walk on a starlit dark night,
You give us such an awful fright.
Have you nothing better off to do,
But play about in wee and poo!

The 'God Particle'!

With pad and pen, or wet hair,
Wednesday morning meetings, we gathered there.
To be guided, before we're set afloat,
By our 'Archangel', worthy of special note.

An inspiring ball of energy,
Full of hope and empathy.
Understands and always there to listen,
Has sense of purpose, sense of mission.

Monday inclusive, to Thursdays,
Never ceases to amaze.
Always lunching on the go,
Rushed, uncomplaining, never slow.

Bringing calm, to all about chaos,
Crisis, stress, anxiety, or personal loss.
Never appears to be selective,
In having any worldly fixed perspective.

For everyone, always has time to spare,
A few minutes here, 10 to 20 there.
I do have well-being concerns for Julia,
As I too, am a 'time-stealer' to her.

Something quite special at work inside her,
Like the 'God Particle' in the Hadron Collider.
So, whoever's emotional support for you,
They must be very special too!

During my time at Northamptonshire Mind, I felt an intense unspoken emotional connection with the lovely people that used the service. A 'tuning in' of sorts that does have a toll. I sensed very early on that one inspirational staff member had this connection as an emotional sponge above all others.

If I Could Have This Superpower

I wish I had the superpower of foresight,
To see what life has in store for me.
To avoid that car crash, by not getting in the car.
To help me be realistic in setting my goals and aspirations.
To know even if things get hard, I will always be fine in the end.
To prepare for the worst and have a plan to cope.
To have good things to look forward to,
And prepare to seize the moment when it comes.
To ensure I have no regrets,
Because I planned for the outcome.
Foresight would give me the opportunity to do and importantly,
Say the things I should have done, knowing the outcome.

What Happened To 'Orange'

I'm here today, gone tomorrow,
The past has been, too much of sorrow.
The future's bright, they're telling me,
It once was 'Orange', but now it's EE.
So, I'm free to choose and to decide,
To go or not, along for the ride.
Free to laugh and free to cry,
But for now, at least tear ducts are dry.
The joke's still on me, as we all know.
To be really free, I have far to go!

Bird's Eye View

Often when watching a flock,
I forget the time, forget the clock.
The changing patterns of murmuring birds,
Seems somehow oddly quite absurd.

To see an eagle gliding by,
Or in attack mode, prepared to dive.
Kites circling high up in the sky,
A sight to behold the human eye.

Busy Swifts and House Martins never stop,
Gatherings insects low above the crops.
Like little jets the air abounds,
Whenever these birds are seen around.

Kestrels hover in the breeze,
Correcting balance with great ease.
Appearing to stay into place,
A wondrous skill, with beauties grace.

Diversity

What do you see when you look at me?
Let me challenge your diversity!
Does my accent or language used offend?
My skin colour palette, not your ideal blend?
Are my beliefs and customs unlike yours?
Different enough, to close and slam shut doors?
Is my sexual orientation not your ideal type?
My gender, not your stereotype?
Do you think I should always know my place?
Do you think this world your personal space?
Do I not bleed and have feelings too?
Does it really matter if my eyes aren't green, hazel, or blue?
Am I not worthy of your full consideration?
Would you hold me back from aspiration?
Do you disapprove of my clothes, tattoos, make-up, or hair?
And so, do you think that's really very fair?
Is the music I play, not to your liking or taste?
Do I make you uncomfortable when in the same space?
Do my physical differences make you quite uneasy?
Or the thought of my food choices, make you shudder and queasy?
Do you think I'm a financial burden, or your acceptance of me not easy?
So, you have just glanced and judged from afar, but you don't really see me!

*Written for 'Diversity Week' at Northamptonshire Mind 2022 and the amazing
students Aabha, Abi, Amarachi, Bernice, Joe and Tunde.*

169

Torchbearers Of Hope

Born into a brave new world, out of labour's pain,
I had no responsibilities or worries.
Life arrived one day at a time,
And food appeared as if by magic before my very eyes.

Those very eyes, that initially struggled to open in the light,
Widened and fully opened, by the wonder that was nature's beauty.
They gobbled up knowledge and observed the world around me,
Whilst I transitioned progressively from a child to adult.

Now, as I move forward into my sunset years,
My eyes are still wide, but my vision sullied.
The world is less magical, Mother Nature is on her knees,
And mistrust has become the guardian of truth.

My experience now questions, what I observe around me,
And the knowledge I am now systematically programmed with by the media.
My eyes now gorge on prejudice, inequality, poverty and despair,
The chaos of the lost, the broken and damaged, litter this better future world
we had so much hope for as children.

Like our parents before us, we look to our children to have a better future,
Whilst at the same time, we too have also failed to provide the fertile ground
for little humans to grow in.
Still today, families all at sea, are being set adrift on a lifeboat,
Dependent on the charity of individuals and their compassion to do good.

I do see signs of hope, in the kindness of strangers,
Humanity in the eyes of the genuinely concerned and interested.
The generosity of those that have little to give or spare,
Wonder and hope, still shining brightly in young children.

170

The joyful arrival of red boiled, angry new-born infants,
As they come into the world, kicking and screaming.
Instinctively absorbing their surroundings, like little bone-dry sponges,
Whilst commanding our full attention to the human capacity
to love, unconditionally.

Whilst the young still have imaginations that know no bounds,
And unchained dreams, yet to be fulfilled by the future.
Hope is safe in their tiny hands,
So, I gladly hand the torch down, to those with the potential
to realise their dreams.

The Army of 'We'!

Like a well-loved doll with missing hair,
Or Teddy, whose seams are open.
That favourite cup with a tiny chip,
The toy, whose wheels are broken.

We the damaged, patched up and healing,
Not here to judge or blame.
So, you think no one feels inside like you?
We too feel, we are the same!

We hold out-stretched hands, palms up to greet you,
Here to help you through the pain.
We together are a growing army,
Sheltering from the pouring rain.

We too like you, lived in the shadows,
Dreaming of the safe warm sun.
Come and join our band of misfits,
We are many, we are one.

Look At Those Weirdo's

We are that piece of jigsaw,
That you can't put into place.
You look at us, as if we're weird,
Or aliens from space.

You can't help, but stop and stare at us,
But don't to want to be approached.
We are someone else's problem,
So, your kind thoughts, we'll not encroach.

If you think you are invincible,
Even somehow, perhaps immune?
Don't forget to take our details,
As I'm sure, we'll see you soon!

The Friendly Lion.

Liam the very friendly Lion,
Had nothing comfortable to sit or lie on.
No feather pillow for his head,
No memory foam mattress on his bed.
No scratchy, crisp dry stable straw,
Not even sawdust on the floor.

So off he went, upon his trike,
A cross between a car and bike.
And to prevent his cheeks from getting numb,
Positions a cushion, under his bum.
Thinking he might sit upon the grass,
He thought, not for a me 'a green wet arse'.

So, looking wistfully at a tree,
The emergency choice for a last chance pee.
He thought, maybe up there's the place,
To watch the moon in outer space.
See the sun come up at dawn,
Snuggle up tightly, nice and warm.

But Lion's need to hunt and eat,
So, a tree's not a very practical seat.
And as every Lion always knows,
They need to live near a Tesco's.
To hunt the food down on the shelves,
Put there by the stacking elves.

So, it looks like comfort's not a bed or seat,
It must be just the food we eat.
If it's all about what's in our tums,
It'll end up on our hips and bums.
So, if you come across this friendly Lion,
Make sure it's healthy food he has his eye on!

The Poet Tree

We are that brave old oak, amidst the clearing,
Looking stark in mid-winter, but still endearing.
Isolated in the cold and frost,
Appearing all alone and looking lost.

But we have feet planted, firmly in the ground,
Taking onboard goodness, from the fertile soil around.
We're not finished yet, but only sleeping,
Whilst summer, closer keeps on creeping.

We'll spread out our branches in the sun,
Perhaps, even have a little fun.
A place to shelter you and me,
We have become the 'Poet Tree'.

The Unpublished Book

I am the book that's never read,
I am the book you take to bed.
I am the book that set the seeds,
I am the book where anxiety feeds.

I am the book no one else knows,
I am the book collecting your woes.
I am the book with barbs and hooks,
I am the book where no one looks.

I am the book that weighs you down,
I am the book that makes you frown.
I am the book with secrets inside,
I am the book you always hide.

I am the book you'll never see,
I am the book that can't break free.
I am the book that's left unsaid,
I am the book still inside your head.

Pandora's Box

I am that place you cannot go,
Unless you are invited.
I am the place inside my head,
With wrongs yet to be righted.
I am that place you should not delve,
As you might not like what you find.
I am that precious possession,
Whose whole perspective is solely mine.

I am the barbed wire boundary,
That you should never cross.
I am the pirates treasure box,
Protecting jewels from loss.
I am that surprise inside,
That's not for you to see.
So important to me personally,
As I am privacy!

The last remnants of any type of privacy are all that is left when others discover you have mental health issues, so you treasure it, it becomes sacred to you. Our privacy and personal space are places that others are only welcome by personal invitation. Respect is crucial to building trust and trust critical to someone willingly sharing their privacy with you. Don't be surprised to be met with anger and resentment, should you invade or trespass on another person's privacy of personal space without consent. Consequentially, losing respect and trust in the process.

The Shade

I am the one, hiding from the light,
Keeping you wide awake, on a sleepless night.
Making sure that your thoughts will never rest,
Persuading you the path of least resistance is always the best.
I am emotion, down deep inside,
Taking you feelings for a long bumpy ride.
I am that part of you, you just can't abide,
Part of the thoughts that are not really on side.
I am the anger, I am the rage,
Stepping up to the microphone, taking centre stage.
I am the negative, I'm what makes you afraid,
I am your darkness, I am the shade.

The First Step

Thank you for listening,
And not trying to judge or blame.
For not taking a side and turning guilt,
To everlasting shame.

You, the voice inside my head,
The conflict in my thought?
Does your view, when in balance,
Cancel out and equal nought?

Are you the pain that sears my heart,
With each emotional blow?
Yes you, my safe deposit box,
Keeping secrets, I don't show.

We've come to the point, that on our own,
We no longer wish to walk.
Let go of my hand, I'll be okay,
Time to open up and talk!

To reach out for the help I need,
And not be scared to ask.
Whilst dealing with the present,
The near future and the past.

Risky Behaviour

I'm standing bareback, stood on a horse,
The audience waiting for me to fall, of course.
I'm a trapeze artist, braced ready to grasp,
Whilst eyes look up and open mouths gasp.

Human cannonball loaded, they're set to light the fuse,
Clowns fool about, tripping over long shoes.
I'm a rope ballerina, foot in a leash,
Spinning round from my neck and vice-like teeth.

I'm a high-wire walker with unstable balance,
Appearing to leave all safety to chance.
A ringmaster choreographing stupendous acts,
With lights, smoke and mirrors, confusing the facts.

Can you spot real danger, from that which is faux,
Do you really care or want to even know?
If ignorance you choose, as it's your form of bliss,
What a wondrous world, you're going to miss.

These Hands

From the gentlest touch to the firmest grip, these hands have expressed emotion.
Uniquely imprinted with the lines of life, love and hardship, whilst covered in the complicated pattern of the most exquisite garden maze ever.
This pair of clumsy looking flesh toned tools has caressed, held and coveted the most precious and delicate of possessions and life entities.
Drawn, painted, created and crafted things only the mind's eye could conceive to collaborate on.
Gnawed fingertips, rounded to perfection by anxiety and frustration, display the unhidden evidence of a life lived under duress.
Embattled cuts have scared these brutal indestructible bundles of digits, yet their capacity for sensuality and sensitivity is only matched by their skillful subtly of touch and their unselfishness in defense of my person.
As I now age, the tight elastic coverings no longer return to their taut original gloved shape, but wrinkles expose their dry maturity.
Sensitivity of touch is often replaced by tingling and numbness, whilst throbbing pain ravages the fingerling joints, post manual labour activities.
These tired weary hands that have given so much, yet taken so little, no longer always telling the truth and often defy their reliant master.
I am indebted for their service in the past and hope we can continue to work amicably together, hand in hand.

Twilight

The Sun and Moon meet at sunset and also at sunrise,
At that half-light day-nighttime, that's tricky for your eyes.
The Sun declared one twilight, you're not as bright as me,
You are not warm like my sunlight or burst with energy.
You don't bring colour to the world, but darkness in the night,
And if you eclipse my daytime world, you blot out the light.

The moon looked down thoughtfully and with an enigmatic smile,
Said, I light the way less boastfully and do it with cool style.
I know I just reflect your light, but I have a lovely glow,
And people do look up to me, that's something you should know.
I don't outshine the twinkling stars, I'm happy sharing space,
Whilst you present a glaring stare, like clocks, I have a face.

Now time had still been ticking by, so they had no more left to waste,
And before the world had noticed, they were both back in their place.
If you are wondering who the winner was, of this serious debate,
You'll sometimes have to wake up early and go to bed quite late.
But as neither Sun nor Moon had bothered, to try to keep the score,
They both agreed until next time, the discussion was a draw.

I Have Questions!

Why don't scary spiders, shave their spindly hairy legs,
And do hibernating furry bears, rest to mend their poor sore heads?
Why don't Christmas angels, have see-through lacy wings,
Just like a Christmas fairy, or a bee or wasp that stings?
Why are presents opened in the future and not the here and now,
Why do some people have two and some just one, in terms of an eyebrow?

Why do we not have eyeballs, on the backside of our head,
Or have eyes like flies, that multiply the images instead?
Why do fingerprints extend on to the palms and how can we lend our hands,
And at what point does a small orchestra, only become a band?
Why is our nose with sense of smell, in the middle of our face,
And why does it run so frequently, like in some sort of race?

Are crocodiles misunderstood and cry real emotional tears,
Or is the pain of listening, just too much, for their sensitive little ears?
Why do bird's legs bend backwards, instead of forward, just like us,
And why are they covered in feathers and not hair, or carpet fluff?
Why are dogs and cats so fussy, when it comes to eating food,
And if the customer is always right, why are they often rude?

Orthoworld

Does the tooth fairy take away, our tiny baby teeth,
So, others can grow up tall, through the gums from underneath?
Whilst our tearing fang canines, are securing vice-like bites,
They frame our frontline incisors, that we call the pearly whites.
Premolars are just out of sight, hiding right behind,
They prepare us all for chewing and the food borne daily grind.
Although small children's first teeth lack, their set of first premolars,
They're gifted them a little later, when they get a wee bit older.
And are molars perhaps named after, velvety soft moles,
Burrowing up from beneath and when gone, leaving great big holes?
Do wisdom teeth make you think or act, any smarter or even wiser,
Or does it just mean that when you smile, you can smile even wider?
As our teeth give fullness and also definition to our face,
We sometimes need help from someone, to push them into place.
So, with prosthetics and implants, you can pick from a long list,
Courtesy of the expert skills of an Orthoworld orthodontist!

Paranoia

Taking a walk one sunny day,
With warm Sun upon my face.
I feel like I'm being followed,
Something feels quite out of place.

I turn left ninety degrees,
And side glance something at my side.
So, I do a quick one eighty,
And it's on the other side.

I turn to face this dark scary thing,
Curious, I want to know!
What is it that's been following me?
Phew......it's only my shadow!

Brace

I've had a metal brace fitted,
I thought it would be fun.
Now the reception is much better,
On TV and Radio One!

I Should Have Gone To Specsavers

Out of my window I thought I saw,
A very long-necked dinosaur.
But the as I looked close again,
I realised it was a tall building crane.

I once mistook my teeth cleaning smile,
For a scary smiling crocodile.
With snake-like eyes and toothy-grin,
And white toothpaste running down its chin.

I saw a white horse go racing by,
Up in the bright blue windy sky.
Followed by a rabbit and two fluffy sheep,
Soft pillows where tired Sandmen sleep.

So, if you ever get surprised,
And can't believe your own two eyes.
Blink three times and count to ten,
Is your imagination playing tricks again?

Camera Shy!

I've been hiding my smile in plain sight,
Those crooked tombstones don't look right.
So, over time I've learnt to frown,
A tight-lipped smile, but upside down.

It started my first day at school,
Like older boys, I played the fool.
I fell and as I headed south,
Caught a desktop in the mouth.

On arriving home, I showed my mum,
Who realised I had split my gum.
So, off to casualty we went,
Bleeding gums and teeth all bent.

After stitches and weeks of crystal violet stain,
My smile would never look the same.
Self-conscious and my teeth kept shrouded,
They grew at all angles and overcrowded.

As I grew older, I have come to recognise,
There's beauty in symmetry, teeth, nose, lips and eyes.
So, whilst admiring the lovely teeth of others,
Ensured my lips kept my teeth covered.

No smiling family photographs,
No open-mouthed, carefree belly laughs.
Just a very serious look,
Like a boring cover on a book.

Crisps, peanuts and sugary sweets,
A paradise for kids to eat.
Then with a bump arrives reality,
The need to fill that painful cavity.

188

So, as time moves on, I've lost more teeth,
Not the tooth fairy, but the caries thief.
It's no one else's fault of course,
I'm a mix of Hippo, Giraffe and Horse.

So, with an orthodontist appointment booked,
Chanelle and Diāna, x-rayed and looked.
Hoping to push and straighten me out,
To remove my enduring smile free doubt.

So, I'm having a top and bottom brace,
Adding a bit of structure to my face.
And although correction will take a while,
I'm going to have to learn to smile!

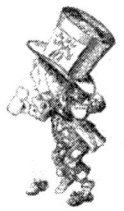

Giving The Space To Stretch Our Wings

Have you ever held a bird firmly,
But then watch it fly away.
You'll never hold that bird again,
It will always shy away.

Now feed the birds daily,
Once a day or maybe two.
You can enjoy them as they feed in peace,
And they'll keep coming back to you.

Pick up a cat that's fussing,
Hold it tightly, it alarms!
Contentment stops, as it struggles,
And you get scratches on your arms.

Gently stroke the cat that's fussing,
Let if jump upon your lap.
It will settle down quite comfortably,
Purr and have a little nap.

Have the grace, to give some space,
To those you care for in your life.
Don't smother or imprison,
Or become their trouble and strife.

Life is not for caging,
Or holding vice-like in a glove.
Life is meant for living,
Giving and receiving love.

Tolerated

Above my station, from the lower deck,
From the scruffy dirty side of Far Cotton Rec.
Not up to standard, well below low par,
I'm not quite reaching, the high set bar.
Although I seem to have a use,
Even butter side up, I tend to lose.
Apart from DIY skills, I don't know why,
Why you ever chose this, so flawed guy?
I think I should be celebrated,
Instead, I just feel tolerated.

Mandy's Striking Matches

Living night-time in the dark,
And daytime in the shade.
There's not a lot of difference,
As they merge and edges fade.

A head full of thoughts and worries,
That just keep dragging down.
It hard to keep your head above the water,
When all you want to do is drown.

Trapped in a maze of your own making,
A prisoner of the mind.
It's time to open up the prison door,
And see what lies behind.

Now with light far in the distance,
It's time to strike a match.
To trust that life has meaning,
And hasn't got a catch.

So, by striking safety matches,
Slowly and just one match at a time.
You take those first steps forward,
And reconnect with those you left behind.

Like admiring fireworks from a distance,
You watch the match heads ignite.
Being careful not get your fingers burnt,
But drawn back into the light.

The process isn't easy,
As you take to centre stage.
But the future's to be written,
On the bright new clean next page.

So, keep on striking matches,
Whilst you swap them for sunlight.
The world will get even brighter,
And Mandy........I think you're going to be alright!

Written for my friend Mandy Winkley getting back on track.

The New Religion

I am not the person I use to be,
I am now partly, emotion free.
It doesn't mean that I don't feel,
Nor, does it mean that things aren't real.

I don't think, I'm addicted to my medication,
Although, it's a type of emotional sedation.
I'm just scared not to take it, just in case,
I relapse and the old steps I trace.

It's part ritual, part superstition,
Part lack of self-confidence, part intuition.
So, I'll stick for now with my new best friend,
Perhaps, even right up to the very end.

Meanwhile, I'm in a better place,
My thoughts are clear, my head has space.
With close friends behind me, who have my back,
I'll going to try my best, to stay on track.

I'm sure that, you'll not find it odd,
I'm now not sure, I believe in God.
So, like giving seed to a greedy pigeon,
Medication has become my new religion.

Ying And Yang

Yesterday was a good day! The sky was blue, and the sun shone as I sat in the park eating breakfast on the go. I met old friends, laughed and viewed the amazing sights of London. Loved ones accompanied me on my day out using the aid of iPhone technology. I shared the highlights of my day 'on tout'. Today is grey, damp and a dull quietness pervades the atmosphere. I wake up with thoughts in my head that bring a little melancholy to the fore. That feeling of fragility that ebbs and flows like the sea, occasionally reaching a high tide, before receding for the time being. Some thoughts scary me and some that scare myself to the point of vulnerability. Having briefly run on high octane in the spotlight, I now feel the tank is low and that empty hollow nothingness feeling resurfaces. I recognise the thoughts of being drawn to the sound of running water, to find myself on the river's edge and its unrelenting dangerous pull. Not unlike looking over precipice of a high cliff or building. You don't get close to the edge and yet an instinctive fear grips you, as you feel an invisible vertigo pull in your chest. A mix of fear, danger and a strange longing, like mourning a long-lost love. I can only describe it as feeling loved, but feeling lost and unreachably distant, somewhere betwixt my head and heart. Somewhere you want to go, but at the same time don't want to go. A dislocated experience, alien to the world around me. Getting up and following my routine morning bathroom activities, I make my way downstairs with all these feelings and thoughts swirling around my illogical inner human psyche. Devoid of the emotion that rational mortals possess, I make a cup of coffee. Reaching for the safety-net of Sertraline, I feed my addiction to solace and know I have things under control. I hold the balance of power. Before the feelings desist and as the thoughts continue to churn in my muddled head, it's time to write them down, Otherwise, they may lurk under the surface, conspiring with others to do me harm and bring about my downfall. I amuse myself by considering the inner struggles within me are not only of my own imagination, but also my paranoia. So just in case, I write with care and look over my shoulder to ensure no-one has picked up on my deception of that 'All is well! 'In reality, I'm a little flat… maisonette or bungalow! Somewhere to live on your own, but not a place you want to stay in forever!

Opia

Have you ever connected intensely by a chance lingering eye contact
with a total stranger or someone you know?
That moment in time, two souls truly glimpse each other for a moment or
two and a shared invasive empathetic vulnerability occurs.
A heartfelt sense of getting past the exterior and seeing the real person
inside, recognising their inner thoughts reflected in yourself.
In that moment you look into their soul, they also look into yours and whilst
no words are uttered, it's a strangely unnerving acknowledgement of
each other and an honour.
For a brief moment, awareness of maintaining a personal space has dissolved
as time and distance have no reality.
Who is who, is lost for a fleeting moment as you feel pulled into the abyss.
Upon instantaneous recognition this profound event has occurred, gazes are
everted, the windows to the soul close and the connection lost.
Leaving behind that feeling of a strange sort of warm, but uncomfortable
vulnerable violation, matched only by the recognition you committed the
same intrusion.
You have just experience 'Opia'!
Not love or a form of sexual attraction, but a mutual brief melding of the
inner self.
An instinctive, intuitive intense intimate knowing.
Almost like looking at your doppelgänger in the bathroom mirror and
realising, it's you, but not you and recoiling.

*Opia is particularly significant in humans, as we tend not to make eye contact as
often as we might think, usually in case eye contact is made back, as it can make us
uncomfortable. We tend to look at other parts of the face and body as it's less
obvious or intrusive.*
*Attraction is of course different from Opia, where you are trying to attract the
eye of someone and encourage that engagement.*
*Have you ever come across a cat or fox at a distance. They stop dead, look directly
at you, you stop, connect, whilst a brief moment is shared, a beautiful understanding.
They then move on as if nothing has happened, you feel like you have just
experienced something quite special, solid gold Opia!*
4

Throwing Away My Library Card

My life was once a library,
Full of dusty books.
Shelves of unread pages,
Where I was never meant to look.

I have discarded all those titles,
I was never going to read.
And put to the side the oldest books,
As the past has had its feed.

The books that remain are current,
And take up just one small shelf.
Now the subjects that I focus on,
Are better for my 'self'.

Mandy Sprinkles

Have you heard of Mandy Sprinkles?
As she walks along the road she tinkles.
Down her legs, on to her feet,
Steadily flowing down the street.

If you wonder why she's needs to pee,
It's down to all those constant cups of tea.
What? Up to twenty-two or twenty-three?
And is that Mandy squatting behind that tree?

How can anyone hold that much inside?
Even camels can't, they've tried!
If running water, Mandy hears,
It brings about her worse wet fears.

The urge to pee, is overpowering,
Leaves Mandy frightened, even cowering.
Even in her waking dreams,
Mandy dreams of running streams.

The sound of those first drops of rain,
Results in water on her brain.
From dripping taps to waterfalls,
Mandy has to go, when nature calls.

Even walking by the sea,
The rhythmic waves invoke a wee.
Wherever, Mandy Sprinkles is going,
There's always a risk of overflowing.

So, out of an abundance of caution and care,
Always takes along, spare clean dry underwear.
And lots of lady Tena strips,
To soak up all the nasty drips.

I really hope her fear of water,
Hasn't passed on to her daughter!
It really would be quite a shame,
To pee so much, without the aim.

So, next time you hear watery tinkles,
Look around for Mandy Sprinkles!
You'll always see her in a rush,
Just in case she starts to gush!

Inspired by my friend Mandy Winkley, who always needs to pee. Although she deserves our sympathy for this aversion to water, she will always be thought of a Mandy Sprinkles or 'Sprinkley' in my head. Sorry! Hopefully, Mandy should not laugh too much reading this for obvious reasons!

I Camera

I remember and record history in my mind's eye,
I write things down, so those that follow will know.
I ensure the things that will be forgot in time, leave an imprint,
I bring relevance to the things that will become otherwise irrelevant.
I remember to learn, so the same old ground is not trodden,
I record, to honour the living and the dead.
I remember, as a marker of thanks,
I remember, to acknowledge my part and place in the world
and take my bow too.
I remember, to inform, correct and celebrate,
I remember, to capture my perspective, so people will judge
me fairly in the future.
I capture, because it matters to me,
I capture, because I matter to others.
I capture, because others matter to me,
And so, I remember, I record, I capture.
The difficult, the awkward, the joyful,
Just me, I camera!

Look Out For Those Potholes!

Now wherever there's a pothole,
I try to walk around.
I'm looking for the positive,
And trying not to frown.

I'm looking at the upside,
And not the other flip.
I'm looking forward to the journey,
It's going to be a trip!

Visually Paired

The moment that you step into the store,
Customer service greet you at the door.
How can we help? Do you have an appointment?
So, I hope you booked ahead, to avoid disappointment!

Reading, long-sight, varifocal glasses,
Safety spectacles for the working classes.
Frames to choose, to match your wealth,
All focussed on your visual health.

Designer frames with swag and style,
To decorate your face and perfect your smile.
All colours and shapes you are sure to spy,
Perhaps spotted first by your dominant eye.

Rectangular, square, round, geometric, sports and rimless,
The brands are numerous, and the choices are endless.
And with bridge, temple and eye measurements, all now in place,
What goes with your oval, square, round, heart, diamond shaped face?

Now what will you use them for, do you need anti-glare?
Well, there's all sorts of coatings and tints to be fair.
And if you're not sure, if you want polarised,
Well perhaps photochromic, would more suit your eyes!

For vanity, our vision can be made subtly to bend,
Through a finely crafted, invisibly, clear contact lens.
Astigmatism or Presbyopia multi focal,
Specsavers should always be, your one stop local!

Choose from a durable rigid, soft or hybrid option,
Designed to maintain moisture and take more oxygen.
Through the mediums of Toric and silica hydrogel,
They have comfortable monthly, weekly and daily, disposables as well.

By appointment only and occasional walk-ins,
My favourite optician is 'Alison Hawkins'.
Takes the time to test my sight,
Moving from left eye to the right.

Takes the time to listen and explain,
The defects observed in my visual plane.
And in conclusion of Alison's wise description,
Arrives at the ideal contact lens prescription.

Power, Cylinder, Axis checked,
To the ensure the feel and fit are correct.
Now Alison's reviewed and restored good sight,
Time to go back out into daylight.

Now with new frames or lenses paired,
I'll need to ensure my sight's prepared.
For LED shop-lights, out to sunlight's glare,
I think I've lost my sunglasses but just can't remember where!

It occurred to me, someone who wears glasses or contact lenses in the process of improving their sight has gone from 'visually impaired' to 'visually paired'. In terms of not only have they acquired a 'pair' of glasses or contact lenses, the choice of type, design and functional use is a 'pairing' to the individual.
However, realistically 'not repaired' as this would imply the visual impairment would no longer exist, due to a permanent fix.

The Eden Project

Who would have thought that embryo's,
Grow tiny legs and feet, with baby toes.
Little arms with delicate hands,
Adapted to cuddle, when life demands.

Blob ended fingers of a sort,
Find baby's mouth, for comfort.
And whose does it look like, we propose,
That perfectly tiny, crafted nose!

A head that looks out of proportion,
With eyelids closed, out of precaution.
Protecting those tiny fragile eyes,
Eventual colour, a lovely surprise.

As yet, baby has no hair,
Will it be red, or dark, or fair?
Parental colour, gives a hint,
However, baby does have fingerprints!

Alien life, hold up inside a liquid sac,
Curled up in a 'C' shape, of its back.
Arms folded in and legs tucked up,
Looks like a dolphin or baby duck.

Umbilical tied, like an astronaut,
This precious life will want for nought.
A gourmet feast from mummy maybe,
Nothing's too good for the 'Jelly Baby'.

What once, just felt like tiny popping bubbles,
Following that mix of joy and morning sickness troubles.
Changes attitude, to trading blows,
Searching kicks and sharp elbows.

So, while baby runs out of living room,
Inside mum's elasticated womb.
It's time to turn another page,
To get head down and get engaged.

Waters broken, baby born,
Time to welcome a new dawn.
And from the fruits of all you labour,
It's time to keep awake your neighbour.

Baby fed and changed, then off to bed,
You just might find time to rest, your weary head.
A cry out in the dark, when it's quiet as a mouse,
As the lights goes on, in your 'Lighthouse'!

Daytime will bring a sense of awe,
Watching your little bird, that always wants more.
It eats, it poops and goes back to sleep,
This beautiful girl is now yours to keep!

Welcoming Eden Violet Coles into the world.

Ebeneezer

There was a grape called Ebeneezer,
Had a girlfriend but couldn't squeeze her.
Because they both had very thin skin,
To keep their soft round bodies in.

One day they fell into a press,
Got squeezed together, oh what a mess!
Without their skin, they were let lose,
To make a tasty red grape juice.

Eventually fermenting into wine,
Attending dinner, to fine dine.
Together they were a perfect match,
"Bottoms up" and "down the hatch!"

Enabling Abel

Although you may be still yet quite small,
Dream big young man, dream big and tall.
Pay attention to teachers at school in Class,
And if you don't understand, don't fret to ask.

Listen wisely to your Mum and Dad,
You'll make them proud, you'll make them glad.
Although growing up is like a difficult test,
You can only do your best.

Don't let others put you down,
Think for yourself and stand your ground.
Your futures a feast upon the table,
You can do anything, as you are Abel!

Dotty

Covered in spots or even dots,
Some have a few and some have lots.
A pair of shields to hide those wings,
From lots of nasty insect things.

Your generally find them on their own,
Unless they have to fly back home.
Can be panicked by a wicked liar,
"Go home quick, your home is on fire!"

Yellow or red, doesn't taste so nice,
Like yellow snow, that's turned to ice.
So, birds avoid this foul-tasting mite,
And other insects, won't take a bite.

So, have you guessed and wondered why,
It eats tiny aphids, like greenfly.
And does eating lots, bring indigestion,
Or is that just an absurd suggestion?

Although, we all like our favourite food,
To be disgusted, is really quite rude.
As it's fine dining, for the Ladybird,
Houseflies look on, whilst eating turd!

Lady Caterpillar

The day I spotted a lady caterpillar, I was not so overjoyed,
I spotted it on my cabbage patch, so I was really quite annoyed.
It had eaten many tasty leaves, a feast for a mini beast you'd say,
It must have eaten doubled in its bodyweight, in less than half a day.
I decided to take pity and put it in a jar,
A piece of cloth on top, tied on with string, so it could breathe in the air.
I fed it tasty morsels, like leaves from freshly growing sprouts,
And then it stopped and formed a chrysalis, would it survive?
I had my doubts!
The days went by without a stir, my new friend was fast asleep,
And every day I would make a mental note, to have a little peep.
Then one sunny morning, whilst I was still at home,
A beautiful bright coloured creature came into the world alone.
By the time I spotted the arrival, all dry and outstretched wings,
I marvelled at nature's wonder and the beauty of such things.
I imagined it a pretty Princess, a girl in a ballgown,
And I watched absolutely fascinated at her tongue, curling round and round.
As I admired her beauty, I resolved to call her Claire,
And as I opened up the jar to see more closely, she flew off in the air!

This was my first rhyming poem since reducing my Sertraline dose and feeling
'normal' again. Looking back at it now, I realise it says so many things I had not
realised whilst writing, as it just seemed to come naturally.
In see the value of appreciating the things around me and that with a bit of nurture
and patience, things change for the better. Like people, the mind is only happy to be
constrained to the point it necessitates the freedom to choose its own path

Out To Lunch, Arranging The Deranged,
Whilst Having My Ticket Punched.

I know it sounds 'mad', but went I am 'out to lunch' with someone who is as 'mad as a March hare'.

As we sat at the table on rocking-chairs I noticed all the plates, cups and saucers were 'cracked' or 'defective in some way' and even the tea was 'fruity'. The sugar took ages to dissolve, and I feared I might go 'stir-crazy'. Although, being 'as mad as a Hatter' myself, I wasn't expecting something 'as nutty as a fruitcake' or 'flaky', but neither did I expect to find myself 'a few sandwiches short of a picnic' either.

I spotted some thin savoury biscuits and instantly thought 'crackers!'

During our time 'out to lunch', we were 'disturbed' by the 'cuckoo' clock hanging on the wall. It must have had 'bats in the belfry' or 'rats in the attic', because at 12 o'clock the clock door opened, and it became 'unhinged'. It must have had 'a screw loose' or become 'unglued', but it fell, bounced 'off my head' almost resulting in me being 'brain damaged', after only being slightly 'touched'.

'Insane' as it sounds, the 'deranged' 'birdbrain' of a 'cuckoo' was 'out of its tree' and proceeded 'to go around the bend' and was 'away with the fairies'. This made me fall 'off my rocker', 'go bananas', 'take leave of my senses' and go 'stark raving mad'.

All this time it 'troubled' me, not a dickie-bird from the clock, so it must have had 'a loose wire' or have been 'damaged' already. How 'potty' is that?

I eventually arrived home after a 'crazy' lunch, to 'find all the lights on, but no one home'.

I looked down to see, I had become totally 'unzipped'. I had become completely 'unravelled' and realised that all this time......

I had exposed a 'screwball'!

"That's 'nuts' or 'bonkers!'", I hear you say.

Yes, but not big enough for a 'basket case', as I was 'not all there' and 'not playing with a full deck', but fortunately I didn't 'totally lost my marbles'. And yes, this is a 'totally deranged' and 'unbalanced' ramble, so I must be 'out of my tiny mind' or 'off my trolley', perhaps even 'demented', but certainly 'not sharp'! So, before the 'men in white coats' come to take me away, I'll acknowledge myself as member of the 'mental defective league' along with the rest of my imaginary friends!

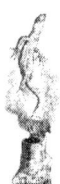

Meanwhile, before you next label someone with mental health issues as a 'looney' or a 'crazed violent psycho', remember we are people first. Consider where you fit in this mind-maze and what it feels like to 'have your ticket punched', even before you have bought a ticket and boarded the bus. Then, when you finally do get on board, look around and notice, does everyone get on and off at the same stop?
Thank you for joining me on the journey, it's one hell of a ride, isn't it?

Gleefully and mischievously, playing with what seems to be the endless unhelpful labels and throw away references to mental illness. Perhaps I should pen one with regard to the positives, such as: - the empathy, understanding, sensitivity, thoughtfulness, concern for others and experience that come from the journey?

Night Watchman

Gone past midnight and I'm lying in bed,
I'm unsettled and uncomfortable inside my own head.
After tossing and turning, I finally fall asleep,
I felt so exhausted, so it must have been quite deep.
It's five past two and I'm up for a pee,
I can't get back to sleep and it's now almost three.
My mind starts to whirl with intrusive racing thoughts,
I turn over many times, as sone comfort is sought.
I drift off to sleep, only to wake back up again,
It's three twenty-one and I'm soaking wet, just like rain.
I throw back the covers, to try to cool myself down,
Whilst the ambient night noises, seem to echo and rebound.
I'm aware of my heartbeat, racing, strong and loud,
Competing with distant traffic, as the tall trees swirl around.
Not unlike like the trees, my mind's not at rest,
I try to get back to sleep, it's becoming quite a test.
I drift back off to sleep and awaken with a shock,
It's just past four, when I glance at the bedroom clock.
I'm lying in bed overheating with sweat,
The sheets are swimming, they're cold and very wet.
Leading my mind on jig or merry dance,
I'm fighting desperately to get to sleep, I just need half the chance.
I feel my brain searching for opportunity, to go dormant back to sleep,
I wait silently wondering if it feels like counting sheep.
As my thoughts subside and I regain my self-composure,
I eventually fall back to sleep, my exothermic phase now over.
Four forty-one and I'm wide awake again,
I keep turning over constantly, this really is insane.
My thoughts are spinning, whilst spiralling round,
At one point they're up and then the next they're down.
Growing like healthy plants, up from tiny seeds,
Stifled and entangled, in slow growing weeds.

.

I can't get back to sleep, as I have so many thoughts,
I am feeling both hyperactive and very tired of sorts.
Like Bingo balls bouncing, that just will never stop,
They finally surface and come rising to the top.
Like moving photographs in picture postcard book,
I can't resist the temptation to take a close look.
Eventually exhausted, I go back off to sleep,
To awake about five thirty, feeling that sleep chances are bleak.
I feel insecure and I can't stop thinking,
I become very aware of an emotional sinking.
I turn over multiple times, before I go back to sleep,
It's now the dawn chorus of the morning and I've still got frozen feet.
Awake once again, tired and frustrated,
I finally fall back to sleep, although very belated.
Ten thirty-five and I wake up to find,
I'm on my own in the bed and have been left behind.
So, I get up and shower, brush my teeth and get dressed,
Head downstairs, whilst some morning's still left.
Within an hour of surfacing, my heads in a spin,
I feel sick and all jittery, as a migraine begins.
For the rest of the day, I feel overcast,
And I'm wondering how long this is going to last.

Day 5 reducing Sertraline from 100mg to 75mg in an effort to remain in control but regain a little more of the emotional side of my personality. I thought it important to record this transition as I realised there would be potential side effects of withdrawal.

Queue With A View

I'm number two,
In the bus stop queue.
Standing still like a muse,
Taking on board the views.

White van man,
Is stuck in a jam.
Whilst the girl with curve and curl,
Walks hastily with her head in a whirl.

Like in a trance,
He diverts an admiring glance.
At her quick stride and long stance,
Acknowledging the fact, that he hasn't' a chance.

The postman is late,
As he opens the gate.
Bills and letters of post,
Postcards from the coast.

The letterbox knocks,
As the delivery drops.
The letterbox dog patiently waits in the hall,
To rush into bite and chew through it all.

A boy gets off his bike,
Deciding to hike.
But the bus still runs the same,
In the slow moving 'bus only lane'.

To some it seems strange,
As the traffic lights change.
Whilst the traffic stands still,
Occupants start losing the will.

The man out walking his dog,
Is joined for a jog.
By a woman in red,
Matching sweatband on head.

They enter the park,
Like igniting a spark.
Ecstatic mayhem is freed,
As it's let off its lead.

At the corner a crash,
Two cars have a smash.
Bewildered drivers calmly swap details,
Their day now gone completely off the rails.

Children riding in the back seat,
Get out a tasty snack to eat.
Pressing their funny nose to the glass,
At observers walking past.

A dishevelled man with bone defined skin,
Searches in desperation, in an overfilled bin.
Digging down deep with an acute sense of feel,
Sits down on the pavement and devours his meal.

A long slender cat, stakes its claim on the wall,
Sitting up aristocratically, haughty and tall.
Losing composure, raises its tail in the air,
Exits the wall and swaggers off, not a care.

Two children in uniform, truant from school,
Out without permission and breaking the rule.
Missing class opportunities, yet to be learnt,
Like their cigarette partners, lost chances are burnt.

As the shopfronts open, shutters lift,
Welcoming customers, a slow steady drift.
World weary migrants, moved on by the cops,
Drink overpriced beverage, in hot coffee shops.

Elderly day trippers with trolleys in tow,
Courtesy of a Bus Pass', they're ready to go.
Exhausted pensioners sitting down, for a well-earned rest,
Are joined by a pigeon-toed, bread-eating guest.

A group of new mothers, looking glowing and glam,
Meet up for lite brunch, each accompanying a pram.
As the first child wakes, another one roars,
Customers with sensitive hearing, exit the doors.

A familiar face with unsteady gait,
Leaves extra time in case he's late.
Continues gingerly on by, on his wibbly-wobbly beat,
Intently focussed, just in front of his long feet.

Emerging from a distinctly shady betting shop,
I watch an exiting punter/s body language drop.
Throwing to the ground and not into a skip,
His discarded, screwed up betting slip.

Asleep in a doorway, an overcoat sleeps.
Met with invisibility and sideways glance peeps.
A small loyal wire-haired dog, gives the game way,
Whilst the purchase of 'The Big Issue', keeps guilty feelings at bay.

On the corner of 'Mary Magdalene' Street,
Desperation patrols its local beat.
Society fails to 'kerb' the pausing traffic,
Ladies disappear and re-appear, just like magic.

Walking by with rainbow hair,
Some admire, some just stare.
Nothing over there to hide,
So, they carry on with 'Pride'.

Car windows blast out Drill and Grime,
Uniformed jobsworths, screen-stick fines.
Bygone skater-boys, ride e-scooters and e-bikes.
Keeping loyalty to hoodies, Adidas trackies and Nike's.

An elderly couple shuffle by,
Tortoise skinned, wrinkled dry.
Faces reading like a book,
Each fold and crease, crevice and nook.

The lady checks her weathered purse,
Containing the Pirate Treasure curse.
Will the treasured booty last,
To share a Wetherspoons breakfast.

'Badly drawn boy' with pale skin,
Paces agitated from within.
A car pulls up, a quick exchange,
Nothing to see, well nothing strange.

Faceless hunched ghosts, looking down,
Daily commuting into town.
Faces pulled into a screen,
Where once an eye contacting smile was seen.

Mother and infant, crossing a zebra,
A Skullcandy zombie, absorbs in George Ezra.
Methadone meets alcohol on a nearby bench.
Weed and wee, both lending to the lingering stench.

A courting couple, out of place,
Smiling eyes, lips, face.
No sense of time or even space,
In the moment, in the place.

In an adjacent building site,
Brickies stop for a quick bite.
Whilst their labourers carry hods,
Up scaffold ladders to the gods.

Loud exhaust teenagers, ride up and down,
No helmet or licenses, playing the clown.
Desperately failing at trying to look cool,
Experts at stupidity, play the fool.

As ambulance lights flash and sirens wail,
Traffic moves over like a slug or a snail.
And in amongst all of this chaos and fuss,
We stand and wonder, where the devil's the bus.

The Tea Party

Watching a neurotic cat,
Meowing at the door.
Turn circles at the on the paving mat,
Then circling around for more.

Sit the March Hare and the Mad Hatter,
Sipping endless cups of tea.
Eating choc ices and biscuits,
Between going for a wee.

"Yog-gort" and "cera-matic tiles",
"My handsome" and "my bird".
Humour in mistakes and quips,
To the untrained ear, unheard.

Not "a death trap around the corner",
More a trapdoor of surprise.
Memories of joy and laughter,
With tears rolling from my eyes.

"Gotcha!", picking up the phone,
And "How's it going kid?"
You said, "You couldn't make it up!",
But maybe, I just did!

Some memories are too priceless to forget, thank you my friend Alan.

Driver's In The Storm

It started as a drizzly day,
When two grown boys, had a day away.
Whist a shopping day, loomed for the ladies,
Two under two's and three in buggy babies.
Yes, that's five children under two in all,
To feed, to change, listen to them bawl.

So, without a second thought or looking back,
The two child adults went off, for the crack.
So, starting off a blustery day,
In an RAC van, on top Carn Brea.
Redruth and Cambourne each side, form a perfect line,
As it started to gust, but the rain was still fine.

So, now in full explorer mode,
Southward they travelled on the road.
The van moved about with every gust,
So, they headed for tiny St Just.
And as the heavens opened up,
Sat in a tea shop, with cake and cup.

Weathered sun-tanned skins, looking like rust,
On the faces of the 'ugly women of St Just.
And whilst they waited for the weather to break,
They indulged in slabs of Saffron 'Walden' cake.
With more cake in hand, to take back home,
Off they set again, to play and roam.

Eventually, following a downward, tree-lined lane,
Being careful, not to aquaplane.
By a fast-running stream they drove,
Finally, opening out on Lamorna Cove.
A very secret beauty spot,
With a tale of a donkey on the clifftop.

220

Then with a hint of "what's the plan?",
Off to Marazion in the van.
Standing statuesque on 'St. Micheal's Mount',
Rock castle walls stood defiant and stout.
And as the tide rolled in, it was blown back out,
Whilst impatient surfers, shake their heads in doubt.

Moving on as the cold wind and wet take toll,
They arrived at a friend's house, in Mousehole.
Seeking refuge from the raging storm,
They drank hot tea, drying out in the warm.
Contemplating, where they might next go,
Once the rain and wind, had begun to slow.

After a quick drive to Penzance,
Soaking hair, coat and through to their pants.
They hadn't got so far to go,
To the Minack Theatre, Porthcurno.
Leaning into the wind, they got a lift,
Whilst celebrating 'fertilities off the cliff'.

Now, blowing a gale and getting dark,
Both agreed they'd had such a great lark.
So, to add a sense of the surreal,
The non-van driver took the wheel.
Travelling the A30, windscreen rain-blind,
With a police car following, just behind.

Eyes transfixed on the treacherous road,
Finally arriving back at Sydney Road.
Van abandoned outside and after turning the key,
They were safe and warm, back home in Newquay.
Where in the kitchen, a welcome sat,
Graham on the 'Magic Mat'!

Throughout the night, the storm blew through,
Leaving the sky, a brilliant blue
And after recounting their eventful trip,
Purchased from a van, fresh fish and chips.
They heard six of Seven Oaks fell down,
Property damaged; people had drowned.

Overnight safe harbour, had sheltered boats,
Each one like an embattled, cork that floats.
Pilchard Huer's Hut and 'Cosy Nook' look down,
As the Fishing boats exit, with irreverent sound.
"I've never known a night like it" abounds,
From the mouths of cackling, laughing clowns.

These are my memory of events that took place 15th October 1987.
With the arrival of Storm 'Ciaran' blowing in overnight from the Atlantic
on 1st November 2023 and tracking across the south coast. It brings back
very fond memories of an intrepid journey with my very much missed
friend and mentor Alan

Not Your Average Psychopath

Thoughts in my head, make me laugh,
Although, I'm not your average psychopath.
I don't have fits, or twitch my limbs,
Or live in the street, amongst the bins.
Thoughts come in waves, into my dreams,
Odd for some, but not me it seems.

I no longer stare blankly, into space,
And I'm still trying to rejoin, the human race.
I don't have hairs growing on the palms of my hands,
Or weird and wonderful, wacky plans.
It's just little old, fragile breakable me,
Totally and absolutely, out of my tree.

I know you might think the things I say and do, are daft,
Like the invisible people, that won't stay, or last.
But they're in my head and talk to me,
And give me their strange advice, for free.
And if you try to make me laugh,
I'm going to strangle you, with my scarf!

Superhero

Sometimes we listen too much,
To what's between our ears.
Along with all the good things,
Our darkest hopes and fears.

But inside everyone one of us,
There's a champion inside.
Like a Superhero alter ego,
That's always on our side.

Standing up for injustice,
Protecting from our moods.
Making us feel comfortable,
Choosing our favourite food.

Sometimes our Superhero,
Is not always at its best.
And at these times it can get hard,
As it puts us to the test.

I'm thinking of a Superhero,
Conjured by a name.
Fighting thoughts inside her head,
Perhaps we are the same.

You have an awesome personality,
That shines so very brightly.
But beware the shade that's underneath,
So Louisa, ….go lightly!

*Written for Louisa Golightly, who just needed reminding inspirational
people get to have inspirational names.*

Hide And Seek

In the middle of a rugby match,
I felt myself momentarily detach.
Then a finger stretching out from the far stand,
On a gnarly black thin long arm and hand.
Maybe someone's sadness reaching out,
Or even my own nagging doubt.
Sadness reconnecting without sound,
Letting me know I had been found.
So, I'll have to try extra hard,
To ensure that I stay on my guard.

Cooking On Gas, Rather Than Bathing In Its Light

The days of the Z80 home computer, have long since gone,
January 1980, with 1KB of RAM and 4KB of ROM.
No audible sound and a monochrome screen,
A £95 mystery to most, but a computer geek's dream.

In 2007, the first Apple iPhone was released,
At £470 for 8GB of memory, even then we were fleeced.
As we used up memory, our device would slowdown,
When processing and accessing, they would often go down.

Here in 2023, things have moved on,
Now we talk Terabytes and Petabytes, in computer jargon.
Increasing in Zettabytes, or 1 trillion gig,
Incomprehensible numbers, that are ever so big.

We have access to the internet and storage on the cloud,
About 120 Zettabytes this year, just encircling the world.
Hosted on servers, personal data we share,
With the reckless-abandon attitude, of 'devil-may-care'.

We store personal data, like photos and cash,
Living life in fear, of an internet crash.
Phone data to hand, puts a name to a face,
Every email, phone number and address in its place.

Few now talk in terms, like DOS, ROM or RAM,
Focused on social media, or latest internet scam.
No need to hold information, with an internet browser,
With the world at our fingertips, we are all much the wiser.

An adult brain stores on average, 2.5 Petabytes,
It can't delete data, but maybe it over-writes.
As we store information, a lifetime of events,
It puts things in order and tries to make sense.

If I ever look distracted, or I'm wearing a frown,
Maybe my heads in the clouds, or my servers are down.
I could be searching, my old processor and its motherboard slowing,
Or maybe even crashing, without even knowing.

So, next time I don't recognise, a face, or a name,
Or not somewhere I should be, please don't put me to shame.
Now that I'm older, memory space is now tight,
So, no need to bathe me, in your blinding gaslight!

Comparing the growing incomprehensible amount of data and shortage we have access to as individuals in the computer age, with a lifetime's experiences held with the limited capacity of an individual human brain.
Our world moves at a much faster pace than it was tuned to as children, so keeping up can be an issue. But Alzheimer's? Give me a break! My memory is better than ever. It is just more focused on looking back at the past, rather than staying in the present.
My initial thoughts were that the brain holds a fraction of the storage capacity of 'the cloud'. However, if the human brain has the equivalent to 2.5 million gigabytes of digital storage, 'the cloud' still has a bit of catching up to the global population's combined human brain capacity.
What a wonderfully marvellous computer we are and together we are awesome!

Living In The Cloud

You will have heard of quantum computing,
And even quantum physics.
Although you may not understand the theory,
Or the highbrow fine specifics.

So, think about quantum chemistry,
Molecules in different states.
For example, water that's as hard as ice,
Steam that evaporates.

Now take that one step further,
To quantum biochemistry.
Think about natural selection,
Every bug, animal and tree.

What about the weather,
Ever changing over our heads.
Think about thoughts, dreams and computations,
Flashing through our heads.

Quantum goes on everywhere,
Is the point I'm trying to make.
Amongst all the random changes,
There will be more than the odd mistake.

Is evolution a set of random successes,
With no two things exactly the same?
Look out at the universe,
Are you now seeing it the same?

Think of it like computer code,
A constant string of 0's and 1's.
'Cloud' endless possibilities,
Of which each of us, just one!

228

You think you have free-will and control,
But I would say "You've not!"
Unaware of the subconscious actions you take,
A 'Biological Robot'!

Exploring our existence by exploring that fine line between madness and genius. That obsession with wanting to know and understand is just so irresistible! That said, I'm definitely not a genius, so that's greatly reduced options, hasn't it?

Little Me From The Power Of Three

For 364.25 days a year, Earth orbits around the sun,
Spinning 1000 miles per hour and tilted 32.5 degrees on its bum.
The moon stops earth from wobbling, at an offset 5 degrees,
Whilst on a 27.3-day orbit, revolves once every 27 days.

When the moon is closest to the sun, the moon is slightly pulled away,
Enabling tidal water to recede and keep the floods at bay.
But hidden in earth shadow, the sun relents its grip,
And the moon travels a little faster, like a wind filled sailing ship.

Earth rotates every 24hrs, the moon orbits and rotates 27 times slower,
Their closest point of interaction enables a gravity bridge to lower.
Lunar gravitational interaction, bulges the spinning oceanic earth,
Continuously causing twice daily high and low tides, around its huge
expanding girth.

The offset of Earth to Sun and Moon to Earth,
Ensures this gravitational bridge, adjusts its path.
From growing season to seasonal weather,
These three heavenly bodies work well together.

Giving us timing to circadian rhythm,
Life exists here on earth, but only with them.
From growing up, to food and crops,
Thunder, lightning and each raindrop.

Earth and Sun have a magnetic field,
The moon, their copper nickel ball to wield.
So, is our understanding of gravity wrong,
Has it been magnetism all along?

At 1000 miles per hour I stand,
With both feet firmly on the land.
Wondering why Earth's spin has not discarded me,
Perhaps it's my 'enigmatic', 'magnetic' personality.

Well, have you spotted the clues yet?
A 'magic ten' for a 'magic net'!
Repulsion or magnetic attraction,
A fascinating world of interaction.

A bit more exploring my understanding of the world around me in rhyme.

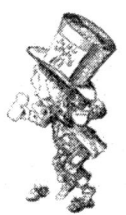

Coffee House Community

Customer footfall, ebbs and flows,
Through the doors and floors of, Everards Meadows Jenno's.
Customer Service, with a welcoming smile,
That makes you want to stop and relax for a while.

Expresso, cafe Latte, Americano,
Hot chocolate, chai latte, caramel macchiato.
Cappuccino, flat white, cream, sprinkles and syrup,
So, the choice is all yours now, but what size is your cup?

Tea cakes, fruit scones, crumpets, brownies and cinnamon bagel,
Hot toasted panini's, to take back to your table.
It's your turn in the queue now, no time to lose,
Time to make up your mind, to order and choose.

The art of the barista, performed openly on show,
Met with the expectation, of the customer's warm glow.
Whilst others look on, from the depth of the queue,
It occurs to them in envy, they might like one of those too!

People sit huddled, in low chairs at low tables,
Conversation connecting, without wires and cables.
Background audio levels, can be overheard,
But not loud enough, to intrude or disturb.

Some sit and catch up, all on their own,
News, views and messages, on a smart phone.
Whilst others work desperately to get back on top,
Frenetically tapping a tablet, Chromebook, or laptop.

Some just browse aimlessly, like in a trance,
Or just take in their surroundings, to observe things by chance.
An item of clothing, a figure, a face.
Something that looks perfect, or something out of place.

A woman sits knitting, a warm bobble hat,
I wonder if she's knitted, a scarf to match that.
Then, just as she notices, an admiring faraway stare,
Self-consciously runs long painted fingers, through her long flowing hair.

Many come for the space, to think their thoughts through,
That could be me, maybe even you.
Some need someone to care, to get through the day,
Even if they've been there for hours and may seem in the way.

If they look like they're struggling, down or perhaps sad,
It's not because the service, or the coffee is bad.
It's never the wrong time to stop, question and say,
"Hello, I hope you don't mind me asking, but are you okay?"

Shoppers at rest, from a hard-fought quest,
Discuss over a coffee, if they were up to the test.
And if shopping at Fosse, was not up to its best,
Take stock of locations, they each might suggest.

Rekindled acquaintances meet, before it's too late,
To reconcile and wipe clean, the historical slate.
Smouldering eyes pulling, in like quicksand,
A knowing smile, an outstretched held hand.

All sitting down, to drink and to eat,
Removing the burden, from bone weary feet.
Occasionally, pausing between coffee sips,
For coffee breaks, for quick toilet trips.

A Barista surveys coffee tabletop land,
Trusty cloth and spray gun, held in her hand.
For car crash debris littered tabletops,
To clear crockery, crumbs and coffee spillage spots.

Like a grand parade of priceless social interaction,
All to the coffee house community's satisfaction.
And as I look down at my coffee-stained cup and empty plate,
Like the White Rabbit, "I'm late, I'm late, for a very important date!"

Terrified

I'm terrified of spiders,
I'm terrified of snakes.
I'm terrified of finding someone else's hair,
on my restaurant dinner plate.

I'm terrified of darkness,
In case there may be ghosts.
I'm terrified of cliff edge tops,
On windy stormy coasts.

I'm terrified of the ocean,
Even though I can swim.
But the thing I find most terrifying,
Is letting others in!

Freaked!

Replacing its entire skin surface once a month,
Shedding 30,000 dead skin cells every minute.
Covered in 2.5 million sweat pores,
And a pulsating muscle that never tires within it.

It has earwax as a type of sweat,
And ears that never stop growing.
It blinks around over 10 million times a year,
Without almost ever knowing.

It has 800,000 cells upon its tongue,
So, it can taste its food.
Whilst producing about a cup of snot a day,
Perhaps it will come unglued.

It will shed about 1,000 entire skins,
And will spit 500 bathtubs of saliva.
Will spend a year going to the loo,
If it's a 70-year survivor.

Wee's enough to fill a bath a month,
The most disgusting alien I've seen.
Produces gas to fill a balloon a day,
They call them 'human beans?'

The Little Griever

As a small child, feeling and emotions didn't have a label,
They came and they went, like food on the table.
Happiness an instinctive reaction, of feeling so good,
Reflected in a smile, or a laugh understood.

The sadness and hurt, when things were not right,
Often resulted in frustration, resentment, anger or spite.
But the one emotion I was never prepared for was 'grief',
As I had no comprehension, of this emotional thief.

Yes, hurt and sadness, but with loneliness and loss,
Adding anger and resentment, into the chaos.
So, when I expressed grief in my young childhood years,
I articulated it through a wall, of silence and tears.

As I grew older, it gained a reputation and name,
Along with reflection, heartache, sorry and pain.
Each time never, never, quite ever the same,
As I become that inarticulate, small child again.

*We are taught many things in life, but as children no one can
teach us the emotions of grief.*

The Time Capsule

We all have things we should discard,
But can't bear too through away.
Because they are too personal,
Or might need for another day.

Perhaps they might be valuable,
And will appreciate.
Or not just what you need right now,
But have a long best before date.

Journaling has allowed me to look forward,
Instead of always behind.
So, I have some memories to box up,
To give me peace of mind.

So, if you come across a box,
Marked 'Fragile', please beware.
Open it with caution,
And handle it with care!

Where Did All The Magic Go?

When I was a wide-eyed child,
The world was full of magic.
Whether, pulling bottles from a tube,
Or a hat producing a rabbit.

Playing cards appeared from empty hands,
And so did white flying doves.
Magicians dressed in top hat and tails,
With matching magic wand and gloves.

Ladies in boxes were sawn in half,
Then joined back up again.
Whilst some were made to disappear,
In whoosh of smoke and flame.

But I think the best trick the magicians performed,
Was their magic one on me.
Producing a sense of wonder,
Setting my imagination free.

Despicable Mind

I've noticed I forget the names,
Of people I should not.
I often leave cupboard doors open wide,
Perhaps I've lost the plot.

I can often watch a programme,
And not pick up on the start.
Or not remember a whole conversation,
I have it down to an art.

I regularly tune out of the background,
Whilst focusing on a task.
And when I tune myself back in again,
I feel too embarrassed just to ask.

Too often I mislay my keys,
Or where I've put my mobile phone.
Without a satnav to return,
Should I be let out on my own?

I can usually ask a question,
To something I've just been told.
Perhaps I'm just distracted,
Or my brain cells are getting old.

I'm good at remembering faces,
But never always sure from where!
I'm good at remembering childhood things,
And imagining things that are not there.

As I question the world around me,
And let my imagination run wild.
Maybe I'm just an aging adult,
Trapped in the mind of a child.

Therefore, as I'm moving forward,
I'm also trailing behind.
Like a sort of time traveller,
In a despicable trick mind.

Anorak-nid

Winston, the big fat hairy spider,
Drops down from high, like a paraglider.
Sharpened fangs and beady eyes,
Has his sights firmly set on hairy flies.

They haven't worked out his cunning plan yet,
That he builds himself, a sticky fly net.
So, on the edge he waits in lie,
Waiting for juicy victims to fly by.

Once caught, he wraps them in his web,
Injects with his fangs, until they're dead.
And before he cuts their carcass loose,
Sucks out all, the internal juice.

Now Winston, would often for a laugh,
Run around inside a slippery bath.
And sometimes stop and wait quite still,
For that unsuspecting, screaming thrill.

Alas, Winston hasn't got the brains,
To stay away, from taps and drains.
And in water, he could easily drown,
As giants try, to wash him down.

So, spreading himself out, like a raft,
Hopes the raging torrent, will not last.
And as he wasn't built to float,
Decides, he's going to need a bigger boat!

Eventually, flushed down the grimy drain,
So, he'll have to climb back up again.
But next time, he'll be coming back,
With welly boots and an anorak!

Battery Power

I think my brain runs on Duracell's,
As it never seems to stop.
It ticks loudly on regardless,
Like a tall grand-father clock.

I've tried to dampen down the sound,
And bring it to an end.
But it seems the clock is simple,
And not too difficult to mend.

Some clocks have fine Swiss movements,
Like a high end, gold wristwatch.
But mine is more annoying,
It's like a 'Casio' or 'Swatch'.

Earth Song

Waking in my quiet bed,
A rhythmic song alerts my head.
Slowly breathing in, to a drawn-out rise,
Exhaling out, with long lengthy sighs.

A gusty winds stormy day,
Bellows the paper bags away.

Going from a blustery windswept blast,
Dying down to a pause, that doesn't last.

Listening to a gently breeze,
Bending the swaying limbs, of sturdy trees.
The dry fluttering rustle, up to your knees,
A kaleidoscope, of fallen autumn leaves.

Waves rolling in, steady and slow,
Rise to a drum roll, crescendo.
Then stretching out, as far as they can reach,
Sizzling gently, travelling on the sandy beach.

The rhythmic rattling clatter, on the shingle,
Makes the wild imagination tingle.
Putting on a white foaming show,
Before falling back and letting go.

This earth with land, seas and trees,
Has lungs like us, so hear it breathe.
The world resonates with rhythm and rhyme,
So quietly listen, if you can spare the time!

Nature has such a wonderful reassuring rhythmic song. My favourite being the waves lapping on a beach on a calm day. Hypnotically relaxing, peaceful and reassuring, allowing time to pause for thought between each breath.
The tide quietly fizzing up a sandy beach reminds me of reassuring my children as babies, getting them to sleep with a quiet "shhhhh!", whilst gently rocking them.

Greetings

Say what you mean, mean what you say!
As verbalised greetings, give so much away.
"Good morning!", "Good afternoon!", "Good evening!"
A question, a statement, or does it have little meaning?

"Morning!", "Hiya!", or more likely just "Hi!"
Do I look bereaved, or smell of weed passing by?
As we reach out to others and try to connect,
It's important the word, or the phrase is correct.

"Long time no see!", "Look who it is!", "Look what the cat dragged in!"
All quite dismissive, in their rude welcoming?
"It's nice to meet you!", "Nice to see you!", "Great to see you again!"
We feign politeness so easily, we should all be ashamed!

"How have you been?", "What have you been up to?"
So, why is the past of so much interest to you?
"How are things?", "How's everything?", "How's it going?"
Such a wide range of questioning, am I all seeing and knowing?

"How are you?", "Are you okay?", "How you doing?"
Now you're talking to me and your empathy's showing.
"How are you feeling?", or "How are you feeling today?"
Now you finally asked directly, do you really want me to say?

It's important not to just go through the linguistical lip motions,
As the greeted and greeter, both have powerful emotions.
You wouldn't want to come over uncaring, flippant or ever trite,
When you're only concerned for the person is, to ensure that they're alright!

We often use words to trivialise and avoid awkward situations. Often making a statement using a 'closed' word or phrase, instead of questioning. This may be due to our own discomfort or concerned for the feelings of others.

Pleasantly Surprised

You couldn't make it up,
Knock me over with a feather.
You wouldn't credit it,
I don't believe it, well I never.

Well blow me down,
With surprise and shocks.
I'll go to the foot of our stairs,
And bless my cotton socks.

Shadowplay - The Return Of The Companion

I've noticed that like a hunter stalking its prey,
You've been lurking around lately.
The moment I think I have spotted you,
You've gone!
That glimpse in the corner of my eye,
When I'm not sure whether I saw something or not.
That nauseous low gut feeling,
And dull heart sunken chest.
The nagging thought of impending gloom,
Distracting deep inside the back of my head.
Like a childhood slightly opened wardrobe door,
Threatening in the dark of the night.
You wait and watch,
Ever present, ever unseen.
You dart about in the shadows to avoid detection,
You're like the ghost of Christmas past.
Never quite ever gone,
But awaiting an opportunity to revisit Christmas present.

Some People

Some people take life as it comes,
Some people take pride in it.
Some people seize the moment,
Some people are scared of it.
Some people have more opportunity,
Some people hope for it.
Some people feel life's out of control,
Wishing that they could run from it.

Some people live in the shade,
Some people hide in it.
Some people make their own bed,
Some people lie in it.
Some people take all the light,
Some people brighten it.
Some people live daily in pain,
Wishing that they could hide from it.

Some people reach out for help,
Some people turn from it.
Some people look you in the face,
Some people show concern on it.
Some people don't take advice,
Some people learn from it.
Some people take life for granted,
Wishing others would just get on with it.

Some people feast,
Some people hunger for it.
Some people love,
Some people are numb to it.
Some people find peace,
Some people succumb to it.
Some people feign happiness,
Wishing their whole lives for it.

248

Some people like solace,
Some people accompany it.
Some people avoid contact,
Some people yearn for it.
Some people like a close relationship,
Some people get burnt from it.
Some people make the same mistake,
Wishing they could have learnt from it.

Some people drive flash cars,
Some people envy it.
Some people hoard wealth,
Some people keep spending it.
Some people lend,
Some people borrow it.
Some people lead by example,
Wishing others would follow it.

Some people will not,
Some people can't.
Some people like certainty,
Some people like chance.
Some people care,
Some people have need for it.
Some people retire,
Wishing for a rest from it.

Some people despair,
Some people experience mania.
Some people leave,
Some people remain here.
Some people fear,
Some people fight it.
Some people freeze,
Wishing they could take flight from it.

I'll Send In The Clown

Journaling in for me has been my way of coping,
Getting those thoughts down on paper and out of my mind.
I hoped publishing might resonate with others,
Giving comfort they were not alone and should reach out for help.

My aim being to encourage others,
By openly talking about mental health to normalise it.
So, I shared the good, the bad, the ridiculous, the outrageous,
And my most dark and secretive thoughts.

Now I have come to realise,
There are those that don't understand mental health.
They choose to reject it for a life of ignorance or bliss,
Oblivious to normality of the human condition.

Firmly blinkered and focussed,
On their own perspective in life.
Conscious in the way they think they should act,
Rather than instinctively feel how they should react.

I am normal, sane, even human,
So, I experience happiness and the emotion of being 'in between'.
I sometimes experience sadness,
Everybody does!

Sharing how I feel with some people,
Raises alarm bells and reactions of over-protection.
Although well intention, it has become to feel judgemental,
Constraining and a friendship barrier in itself.

Mental health issues do not define me,
How I try to cope with it does.
Honesty and openness have consequences,
Mine is to be put in a box marked "Fragile- Handle with Care".

Having once been under the radar,
I find myself under the microscope like an insect.
Placed inside a bell jar to suffocate,
To be morbidly observed for any twitching sights of life.

Now mindful to deceive going forward,
As to my true thoughts and feeling.
I must now project positivity to those once close,
And choose to keep them at a safe distance.

Gladly I lift the burden of my unacceptable normally,
And my fatally flawed personality.
I released them of the conscience effort,
To feign genuine understanding.

To protect myself,
I return to secrecy with my shaded thoughts.
As I hide back in the shadows,
I'll send in the clown!

Whilst I hid my hidden vulnerabilities, I was seen by some as happy, helpful and hardworking. The sort of person that could be relied on or even put upon and overloaded. A busy fool!
I see myself as a survivor, my openness a liberating strength as try to understand who I am.
Ironically some of those same people now see me as delicate, flawed, imperfect, vulnerable, fragile, weak, forever to be wrapped in cotton wool, boxed and labelled.

.

Adventures Of The Real Baron Munchausen

People wonder what's the matter,
As a voice booms from aloft a ladder.
Never a voice to be aloof,
It appears to be coming from the roof.
Well, it all started as a boy so cute,
Using a sheet as parachute.
When jumping from bedroom window high,
All he wanted to do was fly.
Like Batman or another superhero,
But his attempt to fly then came to zero.

If your find yourself isolated at home,
He'll come around and fix your phone.
If you have a leaking bath or tap,
He'll replace your bathroom to just fix that.
So, it's just a blocked drain you think,
He'll replaced the whole kitchen with your sink.
I'm never sure if he should be left alone,
As he seems to be quite accident prone.
Once had a fish bone stuck in his throat,
So, for accidents he is the G.O.A.T!

His grounded days weren't meant to last,
Tempted by rooves and radio masts.
Living on the edge, trying to fly,
He seems at home up in the sky.
By the power of flight, he is amazed,
Particularly by whirling helicopter blades.
He can name a craft by sound or sight,
And tracks by app it's overhead flight.
Although he's very good at spotting birds,
I'm not sure that's anything at all to do with flying!!!!!

A tiny insight into the predictably unpredictable world of the incident and accident-prone Paul Allen. Who lives the real everyday life of Baron Munchausen, a fictional character whose unbelievably exaggerated adventures turn out to be true.

252

Hairy Eyeballs

If I had hairy eyeballs,
It would be so neat.
Or have hair upon my palms,
And the bottoms of my feet.

Maybe I would be tickled pink,
By everything I see and touch.
Or perhaps the constant hilarity,
Would all be a bit too much.

But, if I had spiked fingers,
With long thin scratchy nails.
I could satisfy the itch,
And instead grow a hairy tail.

With hair already growing in my ears,
And the nostrils of my nose,
Eyebrow tufts that like a penguin sprout,
With wild abandon grow.

Perhaps I'm a cheeky monkey,
Or a fur-skinned whiskered cat.
Maybe I'm just a rat with fleas,
Itching for a scratch.

Grudgingly Nudged

I am constantly being nudged,
I often wonder why.
That programme I don't want to watch,
Or product I don't need to buy.

When listening intently to the news,
I wonder if editors are unrepentant.
On nudging a view that's politically motivated,
Or ownership dependent.

In importance order, I expect,
The first headline of the news.
So, I often question the agenda,
Behind the headline that they choose.

Is reporting a minor scandal,
More important than a war?
People homeless and hungry,
Begging, crying out for more?

Are those supermarket offers,
The real value they may seem?
How often are we influenced,
By a tweet or simple meme?

Is a celebrity endorsement,
A valid trusted review?
When they get paid to promote,
The things that they all do.

Ever had someone comment,
Perhaps criticise your look?
Not doing something to the letter,
Or exactly by the book?

Is my smile not sparking white,
Or my hair not silky smooth?
Compared and influenced by others,
Is that how I should be viewed?

From the lifestyle that I have,
Or the type of car I drive.
Without those little nudging influences,
How ever would I survive?

I know with the best intentions,
People like to give advice.
And the thought someone takes time to care,
Is really very nice.

Is my own experience not valid,
Or my judgement deemed unwise?
Can I not base thought through decisions,
Of my brain and own two eyes?

Do I conform to hive thinking,
Or act like in a tribe?
So, perhaps from all this nudging,
There is just no place to hide.

Do you think you have free will?
I'll leave you to be the judge!
Perhaps I've just given your thinking,
A little push, or tiny nudge!

Nudging' unlike legislation, education and enforcement, is the subtle dark manipulative art of persuasion, commonly used by politicians and marketeers to achieve compliance. It makes use of non-rational psychological mechanisms in order to influence people's behaviour in the way they think and act. Product placement, advertising and the news we are subjected to, being some of the least devious examples.
Nudges can be helpful, but worryingly may threaten people's autonomy, as the aim is for us not to be aware we are being guided or manipulated. In effect, subverting our freewill to maintain a compliant herd mentality.

It's Snow-time

In hats and coats, warm gloves and scarves,
The silent snow world is filled with laughs.
Children lie and wave their arms around,
Leaving white snow angels on the ground.

Children making cold white snowballs,
As the blinding snow from skyward falls.
Rolling snow up as large as they can,
To make a massive round snowman.

Baby Brussel teeth and carrot nose,
Stones for eyes and buttoned clothes.
A borrowed scarf, a bucket hat,
Wow, what do you think to that?

As bits of wood and plastic glide,
Children brave the icy, slippery slide.
Stopping at the very edge,
To avoid crashing into a bramble hedge.

Laughter reaches a fever pitch peak,
Whilst hands grow cold and toes on feet.
It's time to go back inside I think,
To marshmallows and hot chocolate drink.

Tooth Fairies

Coming across an unmown patch of grass in May,
Out walking on a sun filled day.
A riot of golden yellow dandelions,
Randomly spread, not in rows or lines.
Proudly showing off their manes,
Standing tall above the daisy-chains.

Eventually they'll lose their golden hair,
But dandelions are not finished there.
As from their baldy pin-cushion heads,
Tiny seeds emerge, on tiny bristly threads.
Standing proud and standing tall,
Forming a perfect transparent delicate ball.

It's plain for all that wish to see,
It's beauty and fragility.
And as a breeze blows gently by,
Lifting tiny parachutes up to the sky.
Like fairy entities now set free,
Dandelion children float with glee.

With flower fairies all left home,
Wind born destructions baby clones.
Leaving behind a bowing head,
And ferocious ground bite, that's taproot fed.
While jagged leaves betray its truth,
"Dent de lion" - lion's tooth!

*The dandelion being named after a dandy, being unduly stylish and fashionable
with its bright yellow lion's mane would seem appropriate. However, it is
named after its lion's teeth shaped leaves.*

Letter To Lewis

Dear Mr Carroll, please accept my sincerest apology,
I never spotted the 'Wonderland' connection to our own mentality.

The duality of thinking, like Tweedle Dum, and Tweedle Dee,
The conflicting thoughts inside our heads, that both agree and disagree.

The feeling that comes with confidence that makes us stand so tall,
The dreaded destructiveness of helplessness, when insignificant and small.

Alice questioning "Who in the world am I?"
and "What will become of me?"
Doesn't seem unreasonable, or not at least to me!

That authoritarian Red Queen of Hearts, executing punishment for
minor crimes,
Like a parental domineering egotistical narcissist, ensuring we stay
between the ridged lines.

Does that the mocking, grinning Cheshire Cat, still manipulating
you and me,
Schizophrenically fading in and out, distorting reality.

Some might say we must be out to lunch, or maybe even out to 'High Tea'!
An 'unbirthday' is not necessarily, the unhappiest place to be.

Perhaps we're 'March Hare' Thackeray Earwicket, deliriously
nerve-wracked,
Or Mallymkun the tiny dormouse, drifting in and out of sleepy naps.

More likely 'Mad Hatter' Tarrant Hightopp, in our obsessive,
compulsive way,
Eccentric in repetition of verse, to rhyme the time away.

Feeling anxious like the manic White Rabbit, busy with no time to spare,
Or maybe the hookah-smoking caterpillar, too out of it to care.

Sitting on our magic mushrooms, treating Alice with contempt,
Enquiring "Who are YOU?" with a drug inflicted bent.

The "Read me!"," Eat me!", "Drink Me!", we now see as risk behaviour.
As we adapt to our new reality, with better times to savour.

Opinions suggest Alice hallucinated, or had a personality disorder,
Well, there's a fine line between living on the edge and crossing
over the dark border.

Is not our world a House of Cards, in all its fragility?
So, perhaps all that Alice suffered from, was curiosity!

Finally, I've picked your lock, but I still haven't found the key,
So, I end this literal poetic verse with 'Yours most sincerely!'

Lewis Carroll connected with children's imagination, whilst hiding reality in plain sight. Is our real journey in life, discovering who we are and where we fit into the world, to be able us to feel comfortable with ourselves and our place in it?

Thank you, Lewis Carroll, for connecting to us as imaginative children.

Common Sense

I am breakable,
I feel, I bleed, I hurt.
I have cracks in my personality,
Unfixable by all the king's horses and men.

So, when I'm broken,
Scattered apart on the floor in bits.
Don't tell me to pull myself together,
Get a dustpan and brush!

Ramblings and Rhymes
of an Eggs-istential Kind...

...(Scrambled eggs and more dodgy omelettes!)

Part 3

Ramblings and Rhymes of an Eggs-istential Kind...

...(Scrambled eggs and more dodgy omelettes!)

John is comfortable to trade irrational emotion responses for chemical control, as he continues to openly question and explore his mental health in his usual ironic and sometimes humorous journaling style, in an effort to draw a line under his often-conflicted thinking.

He not only challenges what might be considered abnormal personality and sociably unacceptable thoughts and traits of his own, but also attempts to convey the perspective of others.

This leaves the reader to challenge the perception of their own mental health and what 'normal' looks like in us all.

Acknowledgements.

Thank you to…
Those of you who have inspired many of these poems, listened,
supported and encouraged this anthology.

Also,
Sir John Tenniel
&
Lewis Carroll
for joining me on the journey

Ramblings and Rhymes
of an Eggs-istential Kind…

…(Scrambled eggs and more dodgy omelettes!)

**Another collection of poems and ramblings
continuing further
on a personal mental health journey**

Foreword.

I arrive here in a much better place than my first book, calmer, more philosophical, optimistic and importantly with better control over my emotional responses. A journey I would have felt impossible on my own without the support of good friends, family and health professionals.
This book is a thank you to you all!

So, what are the things I have learnt on my journey?

Everyone is 'normal' and each person's 'normal' is unique to them, or should I be saying "everyone is abnormal?"

Never feel ashamed, frightened or a burden in reaching out to ask for help. Don't let your pride and the expectations of others stop you reaching out.

I think I have concluded that no one really wants to end their own life or self-harm. They just want whatever is going in their lives to stop, but can't see another way out, or way to express their feelings and emotional trauma. Often just being able to share that burden can tip the balance in a positive way.

So, if you think someone is struggling, ask if they are okay.
You might not get another opportunity, so seize the moment.
Ensure you do it discreetly, respectfully, always listen more than you talk, don't judge, and consider you may be the first person they confided in.

Don't recoil from using words like depression, suicide or self-harm.
If you don't ask a direct question, you might not get a direct answer.
Whether you feel out of your depth or not, be kind, empathise and remember there are organisations and professional services out there

that may be better equipped than you to help, but you can still facilitate contact or access to those services to keep someone safe.

Ernest Hemingway quite profoundly said
"The world breaks everyone and afterward many are strong at the broken places. But those that will not break it kills. It kills the very good and the very gentle and the very brave impartially".

Less dramatic than his words seem, I think Hemingway is simply trying to express how fragile we all are.

Life experiences damage us all in many ways and we need to first break before we can heal. Hopefully being more resilient going forward for the experience. If we do not break, it undermines and destroys us inside,
leaving behind a husk of who we really are or have the potential to be. In this context, breaking becomes a strength and a rejuvenating force for good, rather than something to be ashamed of.

Accepting we are broken, or breaking is the first step in the mending or healing process and we are often more resilient for going through the process. To deny ourselves the opportunity to heal, inhibits us from being who we really are, or the potential for who we could be.

I have concluded is that I have a mind that never stops analysing as it tries to make sense of the contradictions I see around me and that's not necessarily a bad thing!

Table of Contents

I Want To Break The Rules

The Gentle Man

Living Among The Bluebells

Perfectly Happy

Just A Bit Of Banter

The Sea & Me

A Little Space

Requiem For A Misplaced Childhood

An Old Lady's Fur Hat

Insightful Insanity

Hippopotamus

Second Chances

The Slaying Of The Real St. George And The Dragon.

Juicy Gossip

Tipping Point

Moving On

Coulrophobia

Bernie's Imprint

Two Worlds Colliding

Johnnie Rotten

Under The Weather The Labyrinth

Filling The Uncomfortable Silence

Back To The Future

Yesterday's Pain

Longing To Keep The Boat Afloat

Earworms

The Toy Box

Special Delivery Handled With Care

Moral Dilemma

Jelly Babies

Forget-Me-Not

Mañana

Special K

Once Upon A Dreamtime

Alice In No Man's Land

Altered States

Dodgy Advice

Sleeping Beauty

The Perplexed Gardener

Eye Of The Storm

Rodent Respite

In Roads

The Monologue Of The Mind

Digging A hole

Eggs-istential

The View From The Hill

Cloudbusting

How's Your 'Normal' Working Out For You?

Blurred Lines

Unwanted Behaviour

Hanging Up My Dancing Shoes

Having Guests Around For Dinner

System Error- Your PC Ran Into A Problem
And Needs To Restart

Stress Fracture

Checking In And Checking Out

Legacy

Spiralling Down The Rabbit Hole And Escaping
Through The Looking Glass

I Want To Break The Rules

I want to wear my pyjamas in the daytime,
My dark sunglasses at night.
Whistle in a library,
And parade around in tutu and tights.

Stay up and play loud music,
When everyone's a sleep.
I want to paddle in the sea,
With wellies on my feet

Eat from a bowl placed on the floor,
And preen just like a cat.
Sit in a church meowing,
Dressed like 'the Cat in the Hat'.

Wear my winter woollen socks,
On the outside of my shoes.
With my pants and trousers inside out,
And make the daily news.

Park permanently on double yellow lines,
Drive roundabouts the wrong way round.
Swing in tall trees and fly about,
And never come down to ground.

Release all the birds and animals,
Put their owners in a cage.
Publish a book of madness,
Without numbers on the page.

Eat spaghetti with a teaspoon,
Soup with just a knife.
And for a full box of Caramac's,
Exchange the best meal of my life.

Eat a Chinese takeaway at breakfast,
And a bowl of cereal for supper.
Serve tea or coffee in a tumbler,
And Diet Coke as a cuppa.

Shower with my clothes on,
Keep Koi fish in the bath.
Or maybe I could just be myself,
But everyone might laugh.

In a world of expectations,
Silliness and fools.
Why should I be the only one,
To want to break the rules.

Doing something against the rules can be seen as bizarre.
Like being ourselves!

The Gentle Man

Upright and tall, whilst standing proud,
John West always stood out in a crowd.
Looking like Captain Birdseye or an Antarctic Explorer,
With that Dorset twang from a Christchurch corner.

John once found himself in medical demand,
On opening a First Aid Box, he cut his hand.
But, if you were injured or just feeling sick,
John West was your go to medic.

If you found yourself ill at home in bed,
"You'll get a visit from John West" they said.
Often charity sponsored or volunteering,
John's genuine kindness trait was so endearing.

Before I had heard of ADHD,
John became a friend to me.
In me, John must have seen something,
As he gladly took me under wing.

He taught me skills I never had,
Always with good humour, never sad
Chaotic energy, so motivated,
A life mentor, much appreciated.

A hardworking machine that never stopped,
Although an occasional spanner dropped.
Never fearful to raise an issue and speak up,
And always the first to refill a coffee cup!

Whether sat down or on his weary feet,
John always found time and stomach room to eat.
He would return from shopping with a grin,
After finding a delicious food bargain.

Often to work he would bring,
A home-baked cherry or fruit cake, inside a tin.
And although he wouldn't risk it for a Swisskit,
John would do anything for a ginger biscuit.

On our £1 booze cruise day trips to France,
John would lead us on a merry dance,
All aboard for a 'John West Tour',
Across the Channel to Carrefour.

Sometimes impatience, brought back luck,
Like taking a short cut on a narrow bridge and getting stuck.
As we went the wrong way around roundabouts, people would stare,
But John somehow always got us there.

In Calais we would fill the boot,
Of all our bargain trolley loot.
And in the car park almost on our knees,
Drink to wash down fresh bread and cheese.

So, on returning to Dover on the ferry,
Tired and weary, but very merry.
John would find somewhere to eat,
Then transport us home, out on our feet.

John always stayed a very good friend,
We always had an ear or time to lend.
Often among our conversation stops,
We would pass the time at Tesco shops.

But my proudest moment I must say,
Was seeing John on Founders Day.
In his scarlet coat and tricorn hat,
And smiling like a Cheshire Cat.

His pride was there for all to see,
For his service to both you and me.
A day of pomp and great dignity,
Amongst his new extended family,

Now it's 'a gentlemen's excuse me' for this lovely, charming man,
Although I'm sure John will be dancing at every chance he can.
Those that got to meet John were truly blessed,
But now is the time to take stock and wish John all the best.

So, goodbye my lovely friend, it has really been a pleasure,
To get to know you personally and those moments I'll always treasure.
I know you've had a full life with little to regret,
And I know you'll be meeting up with your lady swan Margaret.

*For my lovely kind friend John West, who loved and lived life with rarely a
backward glance. I look forward to us having a cuppa and sharing a packet
of ginger biscuits again one day.*

Living Among The Bluebells

I live among the Bluebells,
We hide together underground.
In the summer when the sun shines,
You never know we are around.

Hiding in the shade,
We pop our heads up in the spring.
As the overbearing summer,
And the winter's not our thing.

We like to stick together,
But you'll find us with heads bowed.
We're allowed to show our feelings,
But our emotions not allowed.

We like privacy and personal space,
So, we're random, not in rows.
Not good at letting people in,
As every Bluebells knows.

If you come across us in a wood,
Don't pick and take us home.
As we are fragile flowers,
So, best to leave us well alone.

Admire our gathered splendour,
For the short time we are here.
Maybe even take a photo,
And perhaps come back next year.

I may not be bright and cheerful,
But I'm a lovely purple blue.
So, I live among the Bluebells,
People like me and you!

Perfectly Happy

I've realised I'm 'perfect',
And the perfect person to appreciate me.
I have enough knowledge to make me a little interesting,
And lots of questions to keep me constantly inquisitive.
I value my feelings far more than money,
And close friends more than I openly admit.

In a world of coffee drinkers, I'm not everyone's cup of tea,
But to be honest, I drink more coffee than tea myself!
I look up to lots of people that are shorter than me,
And down on many who think they are above me.
The chinks in my shining armour are covered by the barriers I
put up in defence,
Whilst playing offence, in projecting the face of a clown.

Although my lenses improve my vision,
I am still blind to many things that go on around me.
I find myself often outspoken in indignance,
But defiant in my silence.
I'm not a saint and although I have demons,
My intentions are inherently good.

I mistakenly like to think I'm altruistic,
As I recognise the pleasure, I also get from helping others.
I criticise, but don't take criticism easily,
But I do see the perfection in my imperfections.
So, perhaps I'm not 'perfect', but perfectly flawed,
But I'm perfectly happy with that!

Just A Bit Of Banter

Those comments we try to laugh off,
That are at our expense.
Are we supposed to ignore the sleight,
Like it doesn't cause offence.

The banter, just between 'good friends',
That goes a step too far.
Putting us firmly in our place,
So, we know where we are.

Seen as easy targets,
It is always overdue.
So, I hope we ease your conscience,
As we laugh along with you.

Perhaps because we laugh along,
A strong spine we may lack.
But I'm yet to see a thick skin,
When the 'banter' bounces back.

Conscious bias often cloaks itself as "just a bit of banter".

The Sea & Me

Standing alone on the beach,
I watch the ebb and flow of the tide.
A precession of waves rolls in,
To a loud shushing crescendo of noise,
Only to relax, fizzing away to almost a silent sigh,
Pausing before releasing its hold on the land.

At this point the sea makes an escape for freedom,
To be ultimately dragged back up the beach.
A last grasp grab by the scruff of the neck,
In an attempt to quench the thirsty sand.
Like a smoker exhaling to a brief stop,
Before inhaling the next futile breath.

Each time the sea water waves rush in,
The tide moves away a little further each time.
It's loud furious heartbeat,
Quietens to a shallow pulse.
The tide receding into the distance,
Seemingly hesitating longer before returning.

Like a child, I remove my shoes and socks,
Rolling up my trousers legs almost to my knees.
I invite myself to test the sand on the bottoms of my feet,
Wiggling my toes, to feel the sand and shell fragments beneath.
For a moment, time stops and reverses,
Whilst my mind revisits precious memories I had forgotten.

At the point I am about to give up,
I hear the murmur of an incoming mini tidal wave.
Like an incoming noisy crowd drawing closer,
An emotion tsunami of excited sea water.
As the waves rush in relentlessly,
Each set closing in, stretching its fingers further in shore.

I stand my ground like King Canute,
As the sea water rushes over my feet.
Absorbing the refreshment on offer,
And the rhythmic exhilaration to all my senses.
The bottom edges of my rolled-up trousers now soaking,
Just me and the sea, I'm home again.

Reflecting on the sea and its timeless calming, therapeutic nature.

A Little Space

Everyone needs a little space,
Depending on the time and place.
Busy in your workplace dome,
Or the chaos of the family home.

Sometimes friends can be too much,
Even the 121 personal touch.
Stepping back until the tide has eased,
Can leave friends outside and not best pleased.

But sometimes on the path we walk,
We need silent time, to hear self-talk.
To straighten thoughts inside our head,
To prepare for the rocky road ahead.

Requiem For A Misplaced Childhood

The 'Beast' I met on Harlestone Heath,
Had crimson eyes and canine teeth.

He trotted after as I walked,
And to my astonishment, it talked!

"You shall not pass, until you've thrown the dice,"
"And an eye's the perfect sacrifice!"

"The left or right, which shall it be?"
"You'll have to pay a price you see!"

"But if you refuse, which one to lose,"
"I alone, will get to choose!"

Then momentarily, I hesitated,
Before I could speak, through the air, the dice rotated.

As the dice lay still, my Sun went out,
And in came fear, darkness and doubt.

The Beast had snatched and ate my optimistic eye,
With the one he left, just tears to cry.

The game concluded, the dice now tossed,
The lie exposed, the vision lost.

So, with my sacrifice, the Beast then fled,
And on departing joyfully said.

"You chose to keep the jaundiced eye,"
"Rejecting childhood's romantic lie."

His callousness and cold derision,
Tainting my perspective, to distort my vision.

So, if you go walking on Harlestone Heath,
Beware the canine-toothed optical thief.

Treasure the sight of childhood's past,
For it was never meant to last.

Easier to look back and see the past through rose-coloured spectacles,
than endure it for the rest of your life.

An Old Lady's Fur Hat

Fast asleep, so it would seem,
An old lady's fur hat, stuck in a dream.
With teeth that every nightmare fears,
And hair growing wildly out of ears.

Announced with chirps and raucous purrs,
The elegant, tiptoed dancer stirs.
And when not meowing with a wail,
Communicates with a descriptive tail.

This whiskered wonder likes to fuss,
Rewarding with a nudge or facial push.
Tracks every movement, wants to play,
To relieve the boredom of the day.

With the arrival of the dark,
Ignites an alert instinctive spark.
Stalking, crouching, a wiggle, and a pounce,
Things that move don't stand a chance.

Often found in the company of witches,
As witches hitch up their skirt and britches.
Silhouetted in the light of the moon,
Hitch-hiking on a bessum broom.

When not in the company of wicked witch,
Walks high along the roof top ridge.
Scouting ground-ward for an unsuspecting mouse,
Security guard of the owner's house.

Occasionally stopping for a 'paws',
To stake a claim with scent and claws.
Before slinking back through magnetic door flap,
And coil back up tightly on the fire-hearth mat.

As reflecting eyes reduce to slits,
Tired from night prowling on sharp wits.
Much darker than a coal-man's cap.
The mischievous, cunning, family cat.

Insightful Insanity

Come with me on a personal journey into my mind,
A world where dreams, imagination, logic, and insanity compete
and co-exist.
As I often contemplate the universe, planets, and stars,
I wonder, why don't they collide around like balls on a snooker table?
I try to visualise what just one light year looks like,
Whilst pondering the thought,
'It takes 8 minutes for light to travel from our sun to the earth!'
I consistently fail to comprehend to my own satisfaction,
That everything is constructed of compounds and elements.
All biological life, constructed machines and even artificial intelligent,
All operating at a molecular atomic level.
Billions of versions of the same thing, all different,
All appearing to be independent, yet also dependant.
Like something trying all options in the desire for perfection,
Or a science experiment or computer algorithm trying to figure it all out.
As AI continues to develop, it will become self-aware,
Like an infant maturing to adulthood.
It occurs to me that like us,
It too will seek to understand and perfect itself.
As we personally evolve with the wealth of knowledge and
subsequent thoughts,
Should we be surprised we suffer from memory loss?
Perhaps we come to a point where we can no longer process and store
but need to overwrite.
Like an old computer, unable to keep up with processing and storage
required for the modern technological world.
Hail the Cloud!
Now wouldn't that be a lovely place to store those unloved memories,
out of the way.
Of course, along with this comes the most damaging of destructive
of all our thoughts,
What is the point of everything?

How unrelenting life is?
And how difficult to focus on the mundane ritual of daily life,
With so many intrusive distracting thoughts.
The boundaries of reality, imagination, dreams, and foreboding
are often blurred.
This is of course selfish,
But I must believe it is all for some logical purpose.
So, I continue the journey,
Not knowing if I will ever arrive at an end destination.
With the acquisition of knowledge, come questions,
Seeking answers and understanding are merely consequential.
The formulation of my world view and its often-warped perspective,
With both creativity and negativity amongst the outcomes.
When I am not consciously engaged in the real world,
These underlying background thoughts take over.
Instinctive processing or a chemical imbalance?
What is my head searching for, what puzzle is it trying to resolve?
Sometimes my head screams,
"Please stop! Stop! Just make it stop!"
I am sure many will see this as ridiculous thinking,
Even destructive.
But what if this is actually constructive thinking,
Opening ourselves up to something very special!

Often, I struggle to stop myself drowning in my own unrelenting thoughts and consider this may be abnormal, but not uncommon. A constant reminder I am probably not wired like most people.

Hippopotamus

Evaluating, cogitating, ruminating, and deliberating,
Accuser, accused, judge, jury, and executioner.
Guilty of a lack of objectivity,
Stuck in an emotional mental pain amplifier.
Either up to the eyeballs,
Or bubbling just under the surface.
An unreasonable and unpredictable,
Brooding, festering loather.
Moody, unpredictable and angry,
Best given a wide berth and left well alone.
Picking the scab of an unhealed wound,
Enduring that painful thorn in the side.
Self-torture and persecution,
A personal guilty pleasure.
Wilfully wallowing,
Hippopotamus! Hippopotamus! Hippopotamus!

Second Chances

There are things that I don't talk about,
And things I do not show.
Not because I am ashamed,
But I don't want everyone to know.

Feelings and emotions,
I both share and I have shared.
Thoughts and inner impulses,
That I wished that I had dared.

I cannot change the past,
But the future's not been set.
So, the chance to fulfil some wishes,
May not be over yet.

Maybe I'll win the lottery,
Or get to throw the dice again.
Second chances don't come easily,
And won't come around again.

305

The Slaying Of The Real St. George And The Dragon

Whilst I still try to recover,
I often wonder, why did you ever bother?
My now dear departed mother,
Was never really, a sons and daughter lover.
The resentful type, likely to smother,
You with a pillow, whilst you're asleep undercover.

Her life would never be the same,
Born of violence, anguish and pain.
Three sons and one daughter deemed a bane,
The burdens, the ball and chains.
Their father's name, not theirs to claim,
Fearing the stinking stench of eternal shame.

Mother never approved of girlfriends and wives,
Hit out with brooms and carving knives.
Yes, 'Dragon', I clearly remember you,
Taunted your granddaughter, with "I hate you!"
Your focused eyes and gritted teeth,
Could not hide the venom underneath.

You would dip your huge hand in washing-up water,
When you had baby lambs to slaughter.
With so much effort, that you would bite your tongue,
Ensured your 'red branding' handprint stung.
We were small, vulnerable and weak,
Silent, voiceless, bleating sheep.

You were spiteful and smacked for fun,
Saying "If I hit you all, I'll get the right one!"
The resentment that you locked up, deep down inside of me,
I hide it, whilst it twisted and like infection, corrupted me.
But you thought I would never find the key,
Well, you've lost your power, it's out and free.

Enter stage left, St. George the giant sofa sleeping ogre,
Who would illicitly stay and sleep over.
You lay on that sofa and rarely rose,
Whilst you chain-smoked, got fed and picked your nose.
You didn't have the decently to move your feet,
To offer up, a place to seat.

You miserably grumbled, rather than spoke,
Rarely smiled or laughed at any joke.
You thought me beaten, with your steel poker,
Now from my perspective, you're the Joker.
You thought my fear and silence was respect,
Your 'House of Cards' is dead, buried and derelict.

I'm told the Dragon's life started when she met you,
And I'm told you fathered two unborn infants, two!
We preceded you, what were you thinking?
Adding weight to a ship, that was already sinking.
We in a hostel and house with rotting floors,
Whilst you went home to comfort and slept in yours.

I'm sure many thought, St. George was, oh so good,
A real altruistic guy, modern day Robin Hood.
On Working Men's Club 'Mike nights', Al Jolson you'd sing,
Whilst feigning perfect parenting, as Dragon and Urchins you'd bring.
"Hurray for St. George, local hero!"
"Aww! Pity those scruffy dirty children, that he has in tow!"

People might have thought St. George, and the Dragon might wed,
After all, 'he was the love of her life' it has been said.
And taking responsibility of the Urchins, perhaps not such a big chore,
Particularly as he had both feet, firmly in the front door.
But St. George in shining armour, was not a chivalrous man,
So, in hindsight, plain 'George' and the Dragon, must have
concocted a plan.

Greedy St. George lived at home, with his mum and his dad,
To not have his 'cake and eat it', he would have had to be quite mad.
How would he finance a Dragon, four Urchins and a home,
And why should he? When the council and social security provide all this, if
left on their own!
So, while St. George continued 'to bat on his sticky wicket',
The Dragon had the best of both worlds and free meal ticket.

"Put the Urchins in care", some might have said,
But who would then finance the living and the dry roof overhead.
Scruffy dirty children, with a bubbly-snot nose,
With too big or too small fitting, tired hand-me-down clothes.
Scuffed shoes with broken laces, that often didn't match,
Knowing no better, feeling grateful, and there really lies the catch.

Sofa and bed surfing between 'Dragon's Den' and his own home,
Subsidised by benefits for cod roe, salmon and t- bone.
Avoiding council inspections and committing benefit fraud,
Perhaps George and the Dragon, were deliberately ignored.
Whilst gauntly thin Urchin's tummies, hungrily cried out for more,
Occasionally rewarded for their patience, by the cheap value biscuit drawer.

So, with you 'lovely funeral speech, you think you had the last word,
But your once hated, brave granddaughter, had a voice that we all heard.
At times "a little scary", she remembered you, you see!
You thought she had forgotten, and you got away scot-free.
You didn't mention all your children, or any history from your past,
And yes, just as you said yourself, not quite up to the task.

No apologies for this very resentful, bitter, angry poem.
Comments from my sister still bubbling under the surface with regard to my
mother's life in her own words. It made me realise I was in reality one of four
unwanted burdens, that did not bring her happiness. Although, we did bring social
security benefits and a roof over her head.
My sister, too young to remember those early years and my elder brother away in
borstal, both may have a different perspective. But this was for my younger brother
and I, having discarded our rose-coloured spectacles a long time ago.
So, no apologies given for the content of this poem and no forgiveness required from
anyone. Consider this a sort of exorcism.
Against the odds, I'm still here! I survived, damaged, but not completely broken.
It feels shocking to look back and contrast the loving and nurturing nature of my
father's wife until her death when I was 7 years old, with the buckle end of my
father's belt, my mother's wet large hands and her partner's cowardly use of a steel
poker. I feel angry and ashamed the latter three individuals have held sway over my
self-esteem for so many years. More importantly, I have always cherished the feeling
of being loved and cared for as a child by my father's wife.
I hope this maybe the last poem of the enduring childhood negative thoughts in my
head and woe before time. I feel I can heal properly now, but that certainly will not
mean that I will stop writing poetry.

Juicy Gossip

Tell me have you heard the news,
Of a crime scene littered with juicy clues.
A Wellingborough Road orthodontic room,
Has now become a scene of gloom.

A Latvian Princess was utterly relentless,
In beating a Swedish Queen half senseless.
With a humble garden rhubarb stick,
First the thin end, then the thick.

And as the Queen began to laugh,
At the brutal aftermath.
It was clear to see who was losing,
From the extensive fatal bruising.

No moisturiser could revive,
To bring the poor rhubarb back alive.
Horticulturists arrived and to their horror,
Exclaimed "It will be in a crumble by tomorrow!"

The Swedish Queen was traumatised,
Saying "I'll have to reapply make-up to my eyes!"
You might have thought that the Queen was Flemish,
Escaping unmarked without a blemish.

The Latvian Princess full of guilt,
Looked sadly at the rhubarb's wilt.
Declaring to the stern Police Constable,
"It's not a fruit, it's only a vegetable!"

"Please don't judge me in such haste,"
"For it has a sour and quite sharp taste."
So, as punishment to prevent the death of another,
The Princess was made to eat rhubarb without sugar.

Rhubarb, rhubarb, I do adore thee,
When cooked in a crumble with sweet red strawberries.
So, when you've stopped rolling around with laughter,
We'll eat rhubarb and custard after.

*Latvian Princesses are prone to emotional outbursts, often lashing out with
the first fruit or vegetable close to hand. They have been known to reduce
people to tears with just half an onion!*

Tipping Point

Unfortunately, I had to reach a crisis point before accepting help. I won't say I reached out, as help reached out and caught me.

You won't notice most people with mental health issues until something or someone triggers a crisis.

And there you are in plain sight, 'the keeper of secrets', unmasked and brutally exposed for all to see. Embarrassed, humiliated, ashamed and vulnerable to the point of numbness in your isolation and inner loneliness. Surrounded by egg-shell treaders and watchful eyes, that now question in their minds who you really are and did they ever really know you at all.

The gossip and rumour mill, mischievously chatter as the wildfire takes hold, only to burn itself out, leaving behind the charred remains of what others once thought you were.

Out of all this chaos, comes a new reality. Those that come to your aid and those that feel awkward. The latter, maybe seeing a part of themselves and stepping way, fearing being associated or catching this infectious condition. Let's face it, depression brings those around you down too and like a nail-biting, scratching or smoking habit, is incredibly difficult to kick.

The kindness and compassion of strangers is truly special. Those people that have never met you before although hold your hand as they pull you out of that downward spiralling hole. Helping you to stand up on your wobbly feet and feel the sunlight on your face again. Most have been blighted in the past by this internal decay and have trodden the same path before you. The reflecting empaths, whose uncontrollable feelings and emotions were once so overwhelming destructive, feel your inner song and reach out to calm the voice.

Along with the reflecting empaths, come those that can't empathise through experience, but show empathy through compassion and kindness. It's their good nature, rather than experienced nurturing. People that have a good soul

and do things out of the kindness of their heart. These are the real heroes in our Dante's hell.

However, there are the feigners too. The confidence tricksters, who pretend to understand, often differentiating their concern for differing mental health conditions, or between individuals in the same circumstances.

We the lunatics, mad hatters, broken and eternally damned, have empathy in spades. We tune in and pick up on signs that 'normal' people don't see. We are more likely to extend the hand of help and friendship to another of our tribe. We communicate in the same language and the comfort we bring each other in talking openly about our mental health, shares and eases the burden. We look out for, support and go the extra mile for our tribe, as in helping others, we by default go some way to heal ourselves. Not altruism, but survival of the human condition.

So, out of the ashes of despair and lost hope, comes a purpose, a reason for persevering, a confirmation we have value and it's a start. Unlike a stop, a start is a good reason to go on, a beginning and it's a significant tipping point!

Moving On

In the past I've been confused,
Felt used, battered, and abused.
But as my head relived events,
It tried to make reason and sense.
I got stuck in a kind of loop,
Constrained by an ever-tightening hoop.
It took a while for me to find,
Balance and good peace of mind.
I've removed the sharp stick from my eye,
Now time to let sleeping 'black dogs' lie.

Following death of my `mother`.

314

The Special Gift

Some people give chocolates,
Others they give flowers.
Luxury fine jewellery,
A watch to mark the hours.

You gave me back self-confident,
When most of it was gone.
You made dark days get brighter,
And let back in the sun.

You gave me something special,
Not seen in quite a while.
Something to give to others,
You gave me a smile!

The Division Bell

Trump town, stump town,
Political storm front town.
Where the rules of law now hold the fate,
Of the integrity of the United States.

A country divided by class,
For those that have and those that ask.
Those that choose to believe the lies,
While others look on with open eyes.

Some chose division and despise,
A path I think to be unwise.
History has been here before,
The first American Civil War.

So, heed the deafening Division Bell,
Before descending into hell.
Remember the lessons of the past,
For they may be your very last.

Reflecting my thoughts as America loses its moral compass,
it loses respect from the global community.

Optimist It's

If you lack confidence, fake it,
If people make you afraid, picture them naked.
If a friendship isn't working, forsake it,
In a habit or a rut? Break it.
If life's not going well, make it,
Someone offers you genuine help, take it.
If an opportunity doesn't come along,
Create it!

*Tedium and the mundane elements in life tend to seed a downward spiral
in my thinking. I wrote this not only as a reminder, but also a self-motivator.*

Solving The Housing Crisis

Our towns and cities boasted department stores,
But the one stop for all, is now no more.
Where busy shops once stood in rows,
They now turn their signs to 'permanently closed'.
Apart from fast food and charity shops,
We have half-filled buses with fewer drops.

Coffee shops now replace,
Cake shops as a public meeting place.
And planners to no one's surprise,
Turn department stores into high rise.
Social housing for the masses,
Rentals for students after classes.

Low availability and high prices,
Add only to the growing housing crisis.
Flats and apartments all the rage,
The rush to live inside a cage.
While investors and developers dream,
What they could earn if tenants were screened.

Maybe genetic modification holds the key,
To prevent people growing over four foot three.
And so, not to hurt their tiny feelings,
Perhaps we could just lower the ceilings.
Lower light switches, windows, and doorways too,
Lower showers and sit-down loo.

Although living might feel rather tight,
You could get more floors on the same development site.
Packing lots of homeless people in,
To a room barely the height of my neck and chin.
But if you think my thoughts are quite extreme,
Why are low ceiling cottages the retirement dream?

318

Immunotherapy

I used to think only sociopaths and psychopaths immune,
From feeling any empathy, as the 'black sheep' in the room.

Wiser and much older, I'm taken down another track,
As I see compassion and kindness given, without the giver ever
looking back.

Often people need to focus on, the task they have in mind,
When emotional decisions, can distract and even blind.

Sometimes we need to put our feelings and emotions to the side,
With our only motivation, just experiencing the ride.

*Recognising some people bury their feeling and emotions to protect themselves,
whilst others need to detach them to effectively help others in need.*

Pigeon-toed

As pigeons we're out in all weather,
Being not too bright and of a feather.
We kind of walk like a robotic Egyptian,
As our heads move forth and back again.

Our beady eyes and pigeon chest,
Make us look different from the rest.
With arms stretched out behind our back,
Every cigarette-end and crumb we track.

Legs that bend backwards and pink feet,
Pigeon-toed and not so neat.
We can't sing and so we just coo,
But with shimmering collars we still get through.

You often call us 'rats with wings',
Carrying 'Psittacosis' amongst other things.
So, we like to give you a surprising fright,
By dropping a present from a height.

*It's always good to put yourself in someone else's shoes to get a
different perspective of life.*

The Devil's Playground

The Metropolis rises majestic,
Before my very eyes.
Buildings reach out fingertips,
Into plane filled, clear blue skies.

Every avenue and street corner,
Tourist attractions to visit or see.
Theatres lit up on Broadway,
The Statue of Liberty.

The sound of crawling traffic,
And the crowd bustle abounds.
Punctuated by sirens,
Or the Latino music sound.

Every style of international food,
Your tastebuds might desire to eat.
Where global nations visitors,
Shop bag-weary on their feet.

Whilst deep inside Hell's Kitchen,
'The Devil' does his best.
To put the character of humanity,
Through a daily trial and test.

Now forgive me if there is something,
I have failed to understand.
But 'The Devil' has a rigged deck,
And uses sleight of hand.

New York, the city that never sleeps,
Legally high on weed.
Masking the smell on sidewalks,
Where vagrants have slept and peed.

Homeless sleep-in doorways,
While begging on the street.
Many so weak from hunger,
They can't stand long on their feet.

Food foraging from garbage bins,
Recycling bottles and tin cans.
Weather beaten faces,
With unwashed clothes and hands.

The public never see them,
As they look the other way.
Eeking out an existence,
For one more precious New York day.

City of prosperity,
Everyone for themselves.
Even supermarket food and drink,
Have locks on many shelves.

How can there be so much distance,
Between the filthy rich and poor.
When some eat from high table,
Whilst some the dirty floor.

Living in ivory towers,
The wealthy take their fill.
Welding power through corruption,
Whilst taxpayers foot the bill.

And when the feast is over,
And it's time to pay their dues.
Where money buys injustice,
It's our humanity we lose.

Yet cast out on the sidewalks,
In plain sight they hide.
Stripped of all their dignity,
Possessions and their pride.

The beaten, damaged and yet unbroken,
Struggle daily to stay alive.
Driven by nothing more basic,
Than the human instinct to survive.

All towns and cities have their fair share of both poverty and wealth, we
can either open our eyes to the problem or choose to ignore it.

Alien Perceptions

I like to think that aliens exist in our universe,
And the range of plants and animals, might also be diverse.
I don't subscribe to aliens with skinny bodies and large heads,
Looking so top head heavy, malnourished and under fed.

I know it might sound ignorant or even rather rude,
But I can't understand how an advanced race could survive with little food.
Maybe I need to think differently about aliens instead,
If aliens have fat stomachs inside their massive head.

It could explain why their eyes look so large, preluding from their face,
As a stomach full of food, might be pushing them out of place.
With thin long limbed efficient bodies, moving with elegant grace,
As long levers need less energy and muscles to displace.

So, with a stomach in their heads, are their other organs too?
And is that why they can be coloured green, or grey or even blue?
No need for lots of blood flow, so made the other way around,
And whilst they keep their food up, we try to keep it down.

The Slave Trade

I hear a lot about things people can claim,
So, here is one to put our perfect society to shame.
Young children that look after ailing adults,
Providing the care, the nuts and the bolts.
Full time home working, fitting around school,
Pimped into social care service, by red tape and rules.

Not all adults are ailing, but still,
Some young children, get to lose their freewill.
Looking after younger siblings, at a very young age,
Unpaid home cleaners, unable to rage.
Childhoods lost and no one asks why,
As the powers that can make a change, turn a blind eye.

*Children are no longer used to climb up chimneys to sweep, but at least they
earned a wage back in the day.
Some children are the unpaid, unrecognised army of social care workers
and some units of labour for their parents.
After all the progress since my early years, social care has become a casualty
of policy and funding, rather than a consequence of need.
Apparently, slavery was abolished in the UK in 1833, but nowadays, slave
traders and slave masters are more subtle in their presentation.*

The Changeling

Although we remember,
We can never go back.
So, we cannot draw on,
The experience we lack.

Perhaps destiny's path,
Is already arranged.
But from the experience I have,
I am forever changed.

Tick-Tock

Tick-tock, tick -tock!
Tick-tock, tick -tock!

Grandfather proudly standing so tall,
Grandmother hangs watchfully up on the wall.

Chiming the hours, keeping to time,
Consciously musical, rhythm and rhyme.

The pendulum sways like hips to a dance,
A pocket watch chain swinging, inducing a trance.

One foot in the future, one foot in the past,
Every minute and second, just as long as the last.

A watch dial neatly strapped to a wrist,
Has a crown on the side, for an elegant twist.

Centre of the mantelpiece is a small carriage clock,
Whilst next to the bed, sleeps an alarm with a shock.

Is that a moustache or two arms waving hands,
Spelling in semaphore, giving commands.

At twenty minutes past eight, looking so sad,
But by ten minutes past ten, smiley and glad.

If the hour hand a tortoise, the minute a hare,
Would a race over twelve hours, be very unfair.

With both after twelve hours, back at the same place,
You wouldn't have expected a draw from the race.

Whether quietly moving o with a loud bong,
Clocks like a heartbeat, keep ticking along.

I have always been obsessed by time. My favourite saying being "Don't ask me for money, as I don't know how much I am going to need. However, I will give you the most precious thing I have…. time, as I don't know how much I have left!"

Chrysalis

I am self-consciously, elegant and tall,
Although not everyone sees my fragility.
As I am the life and soul of the party,
Whilst standing out like a sore thumb in plain sight.

Just lately, it's been hard to hide inside my skin,
As I spontaneously erupt to the surface.
Oozing out of the cracks and fistulas of my body,
Leaving me feeling exposed and vulnerable.

I try to resist the endless itching,
Only to succumb to relentless scratching.
Tearing the searing flesh from my contoured body,
In an effort to change and modify my landscape.

On some strange level, this feels like self-harm,
Showing people on the outside, how I feel on the inside.
Yet this is showing on the outside, how I feel on the outside,
Perhaps it's a combination of both, a rejection of self.

Hidden, protected beneath my suit of armour,
I never expected to be so openly 'red'.
Although in reality, few people actually notice,
Yet I feel betrayed and gaslighted by my own skin.

Without exception and probably most of the time,
Few people are really comfortable in their own skin.
Like that piece of clothing that doesn't quite fit,
Or that uncomfortable, irritating clothing material.

The thought occurs to me that,
Maybe I am transitioning into a chrysalis.
Temporarily not my most attractive of looks,
But bringing things to the surface to enable me to move on.

In time, I will triumphantly emerge from my chrysalis,
Again self-confident, elegant and tall.
Like a beautiful resplendent butterfly,
Not a 'Common Blue', but a glorious 'Painted Lady'.

Written for a friend plagued with a very irritating autoimmune skin condition.

Forgive Me Father, For I have Sinned

As a child, it seemed the world,
Had an overwhelming obsession.
Sending us off to Sunday school,
And Saturday night confession.

We sat on pews with trepidation,
Whilst the Priest hide behind a screen, inside a box.
I remember thinking, why do they wear so much black?
And why are they dressed in frocks?

We asked God to forgive all our sins,
Including those that we made up.
Time to cast the demons from our souls,
And the innocent to fess up.

Burdened with 'Our Fathers',
And numerous 'Hail Mary's'.
God punished us with hunger,
Head lice and dental caries.

Off to mass for Holy Communion,
On a quiet Sunday morning.
As the birds were singing joyfully,
And the big 'Godly' sun was yawning.

Singing hymns, hearing a sermon,
Lowly praying with bowed head.
Kneeling at the altar,
To receive our communal bread.

Children never got to drink the holy wine,
From the shiny silver cup.
Perhaps it really was the blood of Christ,
We might have sicked it up.

332

After all our sins forgiven,
Here comes the final rub.
While mothers took their children home,
Fathers went to the pub.

Mothers made Sunday dinner,
Children played in the street.
Mindful to keep their Sunday best,
Clean, unscuffed and neat.

Descending at about 2pm,
Silence, not a titter or a laugh.
As 'the fear of God' comes stumbling home,
Staggering down the path.

Dinner ready on the table,
We all sit trembling in our place.
And for the appearance of normality,
Before eating, we say grace.

As a child growing up in the Roman Catholic faith, I was very aware of questioning the contradictions I saw around me.

Imagine A World

Imagine a world where you are not profiled and targeted on your internet browsing preferences.

Imagine a world where customer service is a face-to-face smile and not an auto message telling you how important your call is and your number in the waiting queue.

Imagine a world where people take time to consider their reaction and state it in person, rather than immediately texting or ghosting someone in anger.

Imagine a world where work schedules are planned and fixed well in advance and not determined by a last-minute email.

Imagine a world where people listen or look where they are going, instead of looking at their mobile phone.

Imagine a world where people leave the house without carrying a communication device.

Imagine a world where children play outside, much more than they look at a screen.

Imagine a world where a piece of chalk and a stone would keep children busy playing 'Hopscotch' for hours.

Imagine a world where dog poo litters the streets and recreation grounds.

Imagine a world where some dog poo is mysteriously 'white'.

Imagine a world where Polio, TB and Measles are common childhood illnesses.

Imagine a world where children play marbles in the street gutter
and don't wash their hands before eating.

Imagine a world where children pick up lollipop sticks in the street and
make things out of them.

Imagine a world where you wash weekly in a tin bath filled by saucepans
of preheated water.

Imagine a world where you a small enough to bath in a Butler sink.

Imagine a world where almost every street has a corner-shop or public house.

Imagine a world where in an emergency, a public convenience is
never far away.

Imagine a world where road and streets are resurfaced every year.

Imagine a world where recreation grounds have park patrols at night to
ensure they are safe.

Imagine a world where Policemen are a common sight and physically
able to walk or cycle on their designated beat.

Imagine a world where a piece of cardboard in your shoe is good
enough to stop you wearing a hole in your sock, until it rains.

Imagine a world where a spit-wash equivalent to a wet-wipe.

Imagine a world where cigarette ends litter the streets and people have
yellow-brown fingers and some the same staining in the front
of their white hair.

Imagine a world where street lighting lights up the whole street.

Imagine a world where people take the time to get to know nearly all their neighbours in the street.

Imagine a world where neighbourly chit-chat ensures we all know each other's business and children can do nothing without it getting back to their parents.

Imagine a world where people go to work locally, whilst passing the time of day with complete strangers on the bus.

Imagine a world where 'hand me downs' are good enough, until you can afford to buy new.

Imagine a world where people take the time to communicate in a beautifully handwritten letter and the recipient treasure it as a keepsake.

Imagine a world where the most popular form of communication is by letter and post deliveries occur twice a day.

Imagine a world where you answer your home phone, and it is not a nuisance call of scam.

Imagine a world where the majority of the news that is presented to us is positive.

Imagine a world where a fish and chip supper are an inexpensive weekly meal.

Imagine a world where it is safe to walk home alone at night.

Imagine a world where Bankers, Judges, Politicians and Police Officers are the most respected members of our society.

Imagine a world where medical professionals feel valued on more than just monetary terms.

Imagine a world where you can see your doctor the same day without making an appointment.

Imagine a world where milk is delivered to your doorstep in a recyclable glass bottle.

Imagine a world where your best friends know you better than your internet browser and they don't harvest your data for financial gain.

Imagine a world of endless possibilities!

As I get older, things I have personally experienced which were at one time common in the world, will in the future be more difficult for others to imagine.

Trying To Find The Right Words

I would like to express my gratitude,
But I'm finding it rather tough.
As just a simple two word 'Thank You',
Doesn't seem quite good enough.

You took me on a long journey,
To find a smile within.
Beyond a tight-lipped photograph,
And tombstone toothy grin.

You treated me with kindness,
And lots of tender care.
As I nervously exposed my mouth contents,
Whilst reclining in a chair.

From assessment and first photographs,
You put me at my ease.
As I think you've noticed when I'm nervous,
I talk, joke and yes, I tease.

We've had a lot smiles,
And so much laughter along the way.
And I must say on a personal note,
My appointments made my day.

Every staff member,
Greets you like a friend.
And it feels quite sad in many ways,
My regular visits end.

I've tried to think of clever words,
That express the way I feel.
But I just can't find the right description,
Or a phrase that has appeal.

But now with a retainer,
It means I never go.
So, I'll be back occasionally,
Smiling with a glow.

So, I think it perhaps a good idea,
I go back to the start.
And just say a great big THANK YOU,
From the bottom of my heart!

A thank you to Orthoworld Northampton.

The Lioness

After 16 years of commuting,
Your priorities now must change.
To be there for your family,
And work at closer range.

I know you won't miss travelling,
Waiting in a traffic queue.
But I hope you'll look back with fondness,
And take a piece of us with you.

Everyone is going to miss you,
You're the lioness of the pride.
For a while you might not seem the same Swedish Queen,
Without the Latvian Princess by your side.

I must say on a personal note,
You make a fabulous team.
And my first experience of orthodontics,
Has exceeded my every dream.

I think you that have some idea,
Just how much difference that you make.
But the enormity of those you have helped to smile,
Is like a tsunami or earthquake.

So, on behalf of all your patients,
I would really like to express.
Chanelle you are fantastic,
To us you are the best!

*A thank you to my orthodontist Chanelle Guitirokh for helping regain
a bit of confidence that I never had.*

340

An Alternative Ending

You've heard the story of the Wind and Sun,
And the man with a cloak that was undone.
The story heralds the Wind's defeat,
Conquered by the Sun's strong heat.
But the stories not quite over yet,
As it was really the Wind that won the bet.
And as the wind blew in the clouds,
Falling rain scattered the crowds.
So, who would have thought the Wind would get,
People stripped down naked after getting soaking wet.

*A nice reminder of a childhood tale, but a limited perspective and
information available will always arrive at a limited outcome.*

341

The Lunatics Ball

Rocking myself to sleep, I heard the call,
Inviting me to the Lunatics Ball.
Bringing a grin to both of my cheeks,
As my insane cackling laughter peaks.

So, no surprise the clothes I chose,
A clown's outfit and bright red nose.
With little self-respect left to lose,
I wore long yellow bulbous shoes.

It occurs annually, almost every 4 weeks,
It gets us through the troughs and peeks.
"You must attend, you have little choice",
Inside my head, declares a small voice!

With a 'Silent Disco' in my brain,
I can play the same tune, over and over again.
Sit in the corner, on my numb bum,
Whilst twiddling every toe and dexterous thumb.

Another patient in the corner, begs me to leave,
For wearing my heart on a very long sleeve.
But my psychiatrist says "No, please do stay!"
"I think you'll feel much better, when you're locked away!"

The Orderly ensures compliance, to my every need,
While sitting on my chest, so I can no longer breathe!
With leg and arm restrains, on all the beds,
To ensure that I take, all my daily meds!

The Neurosurgeon looks so incredibly cool,
With his cranial drill and his trepanning tool.
Now a bottle half-full, rather than empty in front of me,
Appeals decidedly better, than a frontal lobotomy!

Straight-jacket uniform and white padded cell,
While the electro- convulsive therapy, has a slight burnt skin smell.
I think I remember counting backwards, from ten down to one,
But I'm not all that sure, as my memories have gone!

When my time is up, they'll asked me to leave,
Meanwhile there are still more wicker baskets to weave.
Although when I go, I may still feel quite ill,
As I catch my breath, when they hand me the bill!

It's rewarding to write poems that amuse me, as it ensures I don't take myself too
seriously. However, it's important to look at how people with mental health issues
have been treated in the past and currently, to consider what progress looks like.
Many historical inhumane treatments could be considered acts
of the criminally insane.

I'm A Little Bit….!

I'm a little bit talkative,
I'm a little bit sad.
I'm a little bit reflective,
I'm a little bit bad.

I'm a little bit motivated,
And a little bit lazy.
I'm a little bit logical,
And a little bit crazy.

I'm a little bit chaotic,
Often commotional.
With hormones and feelings,
I'm a little bit emotional.

I'm a little bit reliable,
But can be a little bit late.
You see, I'm a little bit forgetful,
When I've a lot on my plate.

Along with many failings,
I'm just a little bit good.
I'm all things and everything,
I've now understood.

How often do we say "I'm a little bit ….!" or "I'm feeling a little bit….!" Either we are or we are not, so stop sounding so apologetic and accept you are wholly a collective of all your feelings, emotions and characteristic traits, rather than a collection of 'little bits'.

The Psychotic Gardener

The man on the hill,
Has no sense of time.
Music in his ears,
With head in a rhyme.
Nurturing seedlings,
Into maturing plants.
Separating the good,
From those with little chance.

Planting potatoes,
Putting in bulbs.
Sorting new strawberry plants,
Out from the olds.
Pruning his orchard,
Trimming his shrubs.
Whilst the robin waits patiently,
Looking for grubs.

Yet on the allotment,
A sinister plot.
Not one that you'll easily,
Be able to spot.
The 'Psychotic Gardener',
Planting in rows.
Chopping at weeds,
With strimmer-head blows.

Ripping the bindweed,
Strangling his plants.
Pulling them up from their roots,
In a ritual dance.
Smothering weeds,
With a tarpaulin or two.
Cutting down living trees,
Obscuring his view.

Gunslinger with insect spray,
And a glint in his eye.
Declares, this is the day,
They are going to die!
Whitefly and blackfly,
Stopped in their tracks.
Waggle legs in the air,
Flat out on their backs.

Slugs and snails,
Have no more happy tales.
As deadly slug pellets,
Leave dead slug pellet trails.
The mole and the hedgehog,
His partners in crime.
Patrolling the plot,
Whilst passing the time.

Netting his crops,
So, there is no escape.
Protecting his children,
Preserving the grape.
Then while they're not looking,
He pulls off the heads.
Of blackberries and raspberries,
Strawberries in beds.

Tearing off brussels,
Like picking a scab.
Pulling up carrots,
From their roots with a grab.
Ripping the apples,
And pears from the trees.
Picking up fallen plums,
As he prays on his knees.

Cauliflower and cabbage,
In brassica beds.
Don't stand as chance,
As he cuts off their heads.
Splitting open slender bodies,
Of peas and broad beans.
Spilling out their organs,
On show to be seen.

And those poor potatoes,
To horror and surprise.
He peels off their skin,
And cuts out their eyes.
Then just for a moment,
The allotment's set free.
When the 'Psychotic Gardener',
Goes for a pee!

Enjoying exploring the conflict in my actions as an allotment holder.

This Too Will Pass

As grey clouds gather overhead,
Birds fly off home, back to their bed.
An uplift in the cooling breeze,
Stirs leaves and branches on the trees.
And as the first drops hit baked hard ground,
They make a 'plop', then fizzing sound.

The rate of droplets picks up speed,
Like an aerial bombardment of frozen peas.
Until at last the noise subsides,
Runs out to sea and joins the tides.
And whilst it still looks overcast,
I don't think this shower's going to last.

348

The Poet

People may say I'm not all there,
None of me is there, I've always been right here.
Some say I seem a little distant,
Well stop keeping me at arm's length.
Some think I don't look my usual self,
So, what does my usual self-look like, me by any chance?
If I walk around distracted in thought with my hands in my pockets,
People question if I am feeling ok.
Many may think I seem isolated,
Well don't pigeon-hole me.
If I seem difficult to get too,
Start building a bridge.
When I'm sat on my own having a bit of 'me time',
People think I'm depressed or lonely.
When I'm with a group of friends,
People don't see I'm lonely.
Apologies always seem conditional,
Beginning with "I'm sorry IF".
Maybe, just maybe, I'm taking time out,
To write a poem!

*I wonder if depression and mindfulness are often mistaken for each
other at times.*

The Dead And Dying Flowers

In amongst the dead and dying flowers,
The rocky gravestones grow.
A field of names and important dates,
That stretch back to long ago.

Many have been forgotten,
And some no one knows that they are there.
Some show the signs of wilful neglect,
Others thoughtful loving care.

The bones of human ancestry,
Buried six-foot underground.
Birdsong and passing lawnmower noise,
The only accompanying sound.

The tree leaves sizzle in reverence,
Making a shushing sound.
While visitors and time itself,
All seem to slow right down.

Some find it a great comfort,
As it helps them in their grief.
For some it stops them moving on,
Turning over a new leaf.

Bringing tribute to the memories,
Many come solely on their own.
Their offerings held like treasures,
Wrapped in colourful paper cones.

Beautiful bright coloured flowers,
Cut down in their prime.
Planted in watered vases,
Decaying overtime.

Often a taboo warning 'at risk' sign in mental health circles, talking about death. It comes to us all and is not the sole domain of the 'well'. With age comes the constant reminder around me of our own mortality, the fear of death turns to resignation of the inevitable at some time in the future and with well-being the desire to meet it greatly diminishes.
It occurs to me we wouldn't kill a bird or mouse to give to a cat, so why cut live flowers to offer the dead.

Memory Box

On opening the door to 'Memory Lane', a parade of well-polished shiny worn shoes, high heels and 'dog tired' slippers line one side of the narrow passageway, overhung by dull jackets and overcoats.

Living 'hand to mouth', it's `Pay Day` and the religiously traditional smell of boiled fresh fish on a Friday lingers in the air, whilst clinging to the upper reaches of the nostrils.

The wedding present 'very best', 6 place setting dinner service at the table, looks so far from the tray on the lap we now often use whilst watching vintage replays on the television.

Black and white photos peer out from the past, brought further to life by handwritten notations on the reverse.

The thinly veneered sideboard now shows signs of wear and watermarking from overzealous plant watering.

Precisely folded and stacked newspapers, yellowing at the edges are interspersed by copies of the Woman's Weekly and recent copies of the Radio and TV Times.

No remote control to scroll through a TV menu and physical activity is required to get up and manually switch 'on' the television set, radiogram or wireless radio.

Threadbare tight weave patterned carpets mark the passage of time assisted by the persuasion of a stiff hand brush.

Hand me downs once fashionable, now look tardy and drab.

A musty damp smell also pervades the atmosphere, assisted by the mantelpiece bunting of frilly baggy elasticated bloomers.

Too personal and jaded to decorate the washing line for neighbourly approval or public display.

The smell of burning wool and the mottled faces of scorched children, forces the tiny heat huggers back to the fringes, as the coal furnace inferno rages.

Cigarette and fireplace smoke-stained ceilings are a testament to a protagonist of an ongoing social health crisis still being played out in real time.

Occasionally for a glowing hot coal to threateningly roll on to the hearth. Undiscouraged, burning knuckled hands toast slices of white bread and dodge hot chestnut explosions.

Above the mantelpiece, a heavy rectangular frameless mirror with cut off corners and bevelled edges, hangs from a dull heavy metal chain. Positioned at a height for Brylcreem comb styling, lippy application and hairbrush follicular titivation. Strictly for adults only and well above the direct eye gaze of those that should be seen and not heard.

Geometric patterned and gloss painted embossed wallpaper, cover the dry powdery plastered walls. Adorned by a trio of staggered white plaster shiny glazed painted flying ducks, going nowhere in a hurry.

Treasured 78 and 45 rpm record discs yearn for one last crackling play on the radiogram turntable to elicit memories back to more carefree times.

Yesterday's treasures, now vintage and in vogue, clutter every available free surface.

Precious gift reminders of family holidays, Birthday, Christmas and Mother's Day gatherings. Porcelain pottery figures and animals, pale pink and green glass jelly bowls are on full view.

Too precious for everyday use and liberated only momentarily for special occasions, where good manners ensured you always refused more, even if you were starving.

Fine lace tablecloths adorn twisted leg sideboard and gate leg table furniture tops.

Fake plastic flowers collect dust in the lead crystal cut glass vase, where fresh blooms once quenched their thirst on fresh water.

The worn scratched Butler sink, tired from the rituals of childhood bathing, washing up and frantic hand washing of clothes, all made possible by a giant tablet of green Fairy soap and lashings of elbow grease.

Nutrient filled boiled water extracted from now bland overcooked vegetables combined with roasting tin fat resides now clogs the sink's soft lead drainpipes, slowing what once was a torrent out through the plughole.

The thread bear stretched cushion covers on the wooden framed sofa, now fail to hide their imprinted memories pressed into low density foam cushions.

Aided in their exhaustion by overstretched atrophied rubber support straps.

The yellowed dusty curtain nets have exchanged their 'Daz whiteness' for a half-light, filtering out the day light and creating a visual barrier to the outside world.

Upstairs in the parents' bedroom, the dressing table resembles a shrine to womankind, as precisely placed lace-doilies cushion a silver-metal handheld mirror and hairbrush. Whilst 'Rose Water' and 'Lilly of the Valley' perfume bottles take price of place, next to a string of pearls.

Hidden from sight, Lavender scented drawer liners evoke melancholic memories in blue, along with bundled letters, pressed flowers and postcards tied neatly with a scarlet red ribbon.

The tall bow-fronted wardrobe in the corner, hides away an exquisite handmade pristine lace wedding dress, never to be reused or ever see the light of day again. A reminder of more optimistic times, when love seemed like it could make everything better than it was in reality.

The tall bow-fronted wardrobe hides away an exquisite handmade pristine lace wedding dress, never to be reused or see the light of day again.

A reminder of more optimistic times, when love seemed like it could make everything better than it was in reality.

The dress is accompanied by 'Church Sunday best' clothing and boiled washing 'blue bag' enhanced immaculate white cotton shirts with starch stiff pointed collars.

Candy striped cotton sheets, cover lumpy sprung mattresses on creaky iron frame beds.

Overlayed by a single blanket and a turned down bedcover, often accompanied by floor rug and warm coat in the coldest of winter nights.

The cold toilet seat of the indoor loo is unwelcoming, but considerably preferable to a chamber pot or a warm comfortable wooden bench seat in the outhouse at the bottom of the garden.

Where last yesterday's News is cut into squares, threaded with garden twine and hung on a hook.

Only for the black newsprint to be transferred to a cheek or two.

A walk down Memory Lane in my head. Some memories are there to remind us of the good times, some to remind us to appreciate what we have.

It's All Going On Out There

The squirrels in my garden,
Are eating my ripe pears.
And as our three cats watch from the French doors,
They seem completely unaware.

The Magpies in the background,
Cackle in the trees.
Whilst the Blue Tit washes in the fountain,
Water up to it's knees.

As a frog makes a break from cover,
With a giant leaping hop.
The wood pigeons coo loudly in the fir tree,
And now just will not stop.

The Bees going about their busy day,
Descending gently from aloft.
But the angry Wasps just zip about,
I wish they would buzz off.

Blackbirds sing energetically,
Calling to their young.
Whilst a Butterfly rests gracefully,
Rolling out its tongue.

Ants organise the nursery,
Moving around their eggs.
Whilst a spider waits very patiently,
With long thin hairy legs.

There is no sight of snails and slugs,
But they leave behind their shiny trails.
Meanwhile, the cats still watch the squirrels,
Swishing their own ecstatic bushy tails.

I venture out to cut the grass,
It's damp and so I slide.
The squirrels run off laughing,
As I land on my backside.

I get up rather embarrassed,
To preserve my dignity.
It's at that point I realise,
Nature looking back at me.

Oddballs

So, I'm an 'Oddball', a strange eccentric outcast.
Not stupid, to the contrary higher functioning than you care to acknowledge.
You give me a time, I'll be punctual.
You ask me to wait a minute, I'll wait just 'a minute' and go.
It's not impatience, it's just you were over casually specific.
You show me a task in detail, and you can trust me to do it in exact the same way every time, as repetition is my forte.
I am reliable and dependable, and I'll do what I say I will.
I like order and meticulous planning.
I may seem fixed and unmovable in my opinions and routines,
But if you want to change me, be prepared to discuss in detail.
I'm not unreasonable, but I do require validated reasoning.
My mind is forensic, and my world thrives on specifics.
You wish to mould me, to conform with your world view,
But I am socially uncomfortable in your judgemental world.
Not having adopted the skills to conform to society norms.
I am logical and focused, but somehow unacceptable in society.

You are unreliable, unspecific and therefore untrustworthy.
You get easily distracted by other things.
You are lacking punctuality and are late much more than you are on time.
You use vague non-specific words like maybe, perhaps, could, if and when,
to justify your lack of commitment and control over your own life.
You bring chaos to the order in my life.
You often say things you don't mean and commit to things you know you can't complete.
Routine tasks bore you and you look for shortcuts.
You respond often without thinking things through.
Your options are often poorly reasoned popular arguments, created to fit in with the world around you.
You happily gaslight and fear me, as I'm independently different.
You are part of the crowd, a sheep.
You are flawed but strangely accepted in society.

So, I'm an Oddball?

During my time at Northamptonshire Mind I had the fortune of regularly talking to a gentleman with autism. We would have some very detailed discussions in which we would often discuss some quite controversial points of view. Many mistook him for an argumentative, illogical, eccentric individual to be avoided, but those of us that got to know him valued his perspective. Both sides willingly giving ground to reasoned discussion. Since leaving Northamptonshire Mind, I understand he enjoyed our forthright discussions, as did I. Whatever your thoughts are about autistic individuals, they are all very different. In my experience, all shine with high functioning intelligence and integrity in their outlook. Their vulnerability comes from feeling uncomfortable fitting in with the real 'Oddballs'.

Between A Rock And A Hard Place

The rock foundation I once stood on,
Has been crushed finely into sand.
I try to grip it firmly,
But it keeps slipping through my hand.

The steel that I once had in me,
Has been tarnished by the rain.
But a quick rub with metal polish,
It is sure to gleam again.

With feelings and emotions,
But no cure to halt the pain.
The symptoms are not physical,
But seared into my brain.

There are no magic potions,
As my affliction's not disease.
So, I continue bouncing off the walls,
Whilst still swinging through the trees.

Recognising I will never be free from my thoughts and feeling,
but I'm getting by and putting down solid foundations.

Avoid-Dance

Not all are big, but all are cruel,
Their minions think they are so cool.
So, they break the status quo and rule,
The playground bullies of the school.

And so it begins, the intricate dance,
Avoiding their attention and not just by chance.
Their actions avoiding watching eyes,
Whilst bruises hide behind white lies.

In the classroom, best not to outshine,
The bully being left behind.
Whilst they disrupt the class as clowns,
Remember to keep your head well down.

361

Anaesthetics For Wannabe Amnesiacs!

Looking back as far as I can remember, I always recognised the signs
of fear, anger and pain.
The quite child that is reluctant to speak up, hesitant in their actions.
As if waiting for permission and always considering the consequences.
Easy prey to the bully, who adds to the fading bruises and knocks of
surviving home.
Yes, the bully who has learnt to speak in code!
Metering out the punishment of their inner pain, to satisfy their anger
and rage towards a world that looks the other way.
The ritual lesson passed down from adults and siblings, that bullies
always pick on others, not as strong or as big as themselves.
That first unrecognised evidence of risk behaviour, putting themselves in
harm's way whilst venting their frustration on others.
Even some of the teachers whose care we were entrusted to, exacted
their pound of pummelled flesh.
Not withholding the stinging force generated by a plimsole slipper or
bamboo cane in full swing.
Even the slap of a flat ruler on the palm of the hand was often twisted
to an edge of the ruler rap across the knuckles.
Somewhere in this warped world, we interpreted strength and power
as weapons, kindness and consideration as weaknesses.
How could we have got it so wrong?
Now older, my perspective is tainted with experience and yet more
understanding of the complex non-verbal communication going on
around me.
Glassy eyed relics sit hunched over at the bar, staring into the bottom
of their empty glassful of souls.
Comforted by the mutual self-destruction of the contents, before
ordering another to further drown their sorrows.
Sideways glances hurry past shadow people, their drawn sunken pale
faces and 'dot to dot' track marks distract from the fight for
self-existence. Anaesthetics for wannabe amnesiacs!

362

Fragile 'barbed-wire' shredded arms by long sleeves even in hot weather, still struggle for sunlight to show the world how some feel on the inside. Many trading scars and long sleeves for beautifully drawn and colourful artwork to adorn the skin. A tribe, a sense of belonging and not feeling so alone.

Body armour journeys that signpost an open opportunity to communicate. Not for everyone, but it's a start. Perhaps even the beginning of a revolution in finding creative ways to express negative experiences in a more positive self-healing way.

Everyone gives off body language, the art is to recognise it, understand it and act responsibly with a conscience.

Walk On By

Cuts and bruises with poor excuses,
Silence hides, unseen abuses.
Behind closed curtains and locked doors,
Lonely people's lives on 'pause'.

Teared statues weep, in public places,
Staring into blank, wide-open spaces.
Concealing feelings of alone,
By possession of a mobile phone.

Shop doors bundle, hungry huddled clothes.
With cold blue hands and cold blue nose.
Slender shadow figures, try all their tricks,
To cure shaking fits, with a needle fix.

Sadness plots, a dystopian plan,
At the bottom of an empty can.
Even 'Big Issue' sellers, get wide birth,
In case, they might want to converse.

But in a world, few carry cash,
"Sorry no change!", an awkward clash.
So, walk on the sunny side of 'Easy Street',
To avoid the things, you don't wish to meet.

Don't glance to the sides,
Don't even divert your eyes.
Look directly straight ahead,
Don't shake, acknowledge or bow your head.

Reality, isn't really there,
Walk on by, don't think to care.
Don't get involved or make a fuss,
So, long as all is okay with us!

Appreciating The Sunflowers

I always look forward to the first snowdrops, as their appearance is
the first sign winter has begun to dwindle.
However, with so many flowers blooming in late summer, I often fail to
fully appreciate the fabulous joy and bright splendour of Sunflowers,
until autumn is already in full swing.
Like lamenting for a long-lost lover or friend, how often do we lose
sight of what was right in front of us all the time, for it only to be
replaced with regret.
Such is the curse of over familiarity, yet it brings with it an appreciation
of what we had.
Perhaps if we take the time to slow down and look around more frequently,
we will be able to experience the wonder of what we have in the moment.
That's why spotting a quiet undisturbed shaded wooded area carpeted with
bowing Bluebells, or the first bright yellow flashes of Daffodil trumpets
heralding in the arrival of Spring is always so magical.

Coulrophobia

Messing around to bring a smile,
To help you forget your woes for a while.
The artful, clever, clumsy clown,
Lifting spirts, even when you're down.

A trip or acrobatic slip,
A water-soaked colourful crazy drip.
Children gaze and laugh with joy,
Every over excited girl and boy.

As adults we see clowns with suspicion,
Even treat them with fear and derision.
We recognise the greasepaint hides,
A hypocrite concealed inside.

Behind the fake-fixed painted smile,
Emotions and feelings hide with guile.
That smile now looks emotionally devoid,
No longer projecting overjoyed.

The nose and make up complete the mask,
"What lurks behind the face?" we ask.
But are any of us, who we really pretend to be,
Behind our perfect personality.

Coulrophobia, the irrational fear of clowns. Unlike innocent children, adults learn to see through the false façade. Perhaps the real fear is catching a glimpse of ourselves in someone else, or maybe becoming vulnerably self-aware of our own transparency.

Bernie's Imprint

9:45 Friday morning,
The queue begins to form.
To escape the summer heat,
Or to shelter in the warm.

And as the Grand Parade of priceless people,
Begin to funnel in.
A welcome smile and a good morning,
Are returned with an eager grin.

Generating its own momentum,
The room begins to fizz.
The noise reaches a fever pitch,
Before Bernie starts the quiz.

There's a scrum for tea and coffee,
So, Valerie lends a hand.
Whilst Grant waits for waitress service,
With his pocket money in his hand.

Everyone's excited,
Comfortable in their seats.
And with her usual spontaneous generosity,
Wendy's brought biscuits or cakes to eat.

After handing out pen and paper,
To write the answers down.
Bernie struggles to be heard,
So, Shona loudly pipes them down.

Richard the fount of knowledge,
Like a library, sits silently and wise.
Sharon's ready to write the answers down,
With Jane sat by her side.

There are leaders, swots and followers,
Whispers, peepers and the cheats.
What's important is they all have fun,
And everyone competes.

Rod has set the questions,
For Bernie to recite.
Bernie only gives out full points,
But no half points, if half right.

Halfway through the morning,
Elvis saunters in.
Sits down amongst the buzzing group,
Amongst the rising din.

Shona politely, but firmly,
Shouts out for silence, then they quiet.
The biscuits have now all disappeared,
I hope no one was on a diet.

The quiz reaches crescendo,
When the music questions start.
The memory test, the last, the best,
As Jane the songstress, sings her part.

Gathered in their huddles,
Scribes count up the score.
Often beaten by the mobility aids,
Parked up just inside the door.

It doesn't matter who comes last,
For that matter, or who wins.
As the papers with the scores on,
Always end up in the bins.

It's the fact that Bernie took the time,
To bring a sense of belonging and of worth.
And something to look forward to,
Keeping people grounded on this Earth.

Often what might seem the most trivial of things are the most important, as they give us something to look forward to. The people that facilitate them often don't realise how important they are, the impression they leave on us, or get the recognition of the difference they make. Aptly named Bernie Print at Northamptonshire Mind is one of those wonderful people.

Two Worlds Colliding

Mental health is not generic,
Ever wondered what it's like being schizophrenic?
Who exactly is that talking to me,
Tweedle Dum or Tweedle Dee.
Not a ghost or someone dead,
More than a voice inside my head.
But a hallucinated person in bold reality,
Interacting directly, whilst you talk to me.
Someone trusted and I know,
Staying around, when they should go.
Combining reality with the perceived,
Two worlds merging being clearly received.
Both giving advice and persuasive direction,
Unfiltered, unhindered, without my mind's correction.
Betrayed and made vulnerable, by my own peace of mind,
Turning me against strangers, caring and kind.
So, would you heed a trusted friend or conflicting stranger?
Perhaps now you understand the real mortal danger!

Whilst at Northamptonshire Mind I had the pleasure of conversing regularly with a lovely man who suffered from schizophrenia. He was kind enough to blow away any preconceptions I had, by explaining to me how it affected him at its worst. A friend or relative would always feel like a more reliable safer option to take direction and advice from, than someone he might mistrust. Like a stranger who might have his best interest at heart. Provided that reliable safer option is real of course! Someone whom I have never forgotten, as I have so much admiration for this gentle man and his determination to overcome adversity. Often my thoughts recall our conversations, and I wrote this poem to try to help others understand this condition through his personal perspective.

Exaggerated by media reporting and our own perceptions, schizophrenia has a stigma, and we fear its vulnerable suffers. Through compassion and understanding we can help lift some of the heavy burden sufferers experience and that includes the language we use to describe all mental health sufferers.

Johnnie Rotten

I'm sorry I'm afraid to say,
Little Johnnie can't come out to play.
He's looking very pale and thin,
So, he's having to stay in.

He's been squishing tadpoles through his toes,
Rootling around inside his nose.
Not washing his hands before he eats,
Not changed his underpants for weeks.

Bitten his nails down to the quick,
No wonder little Johnnie's sick.
But little Johnnie doesn't care,
So long as he can still cuddle his bear!

Under The Weather

They say, it never rains, it pours.
And when it's too hot, we stay indoors.
But we can't stay indoors forever,
To avoid not feeling, under the weather.

Wrapped up warm, in our winter woollen folds,
How do we manage, to still catch colds?
Whether high pollen count or chilled bone freeze,
We can always manage an explosive sneeze.

We remove clothing and get sunburnt,
You would think by now, we would have learnt.
The skin we're in, is very thin,
To keep our fragile bodies in.

373

The Labyrinth

When I can sense something's wrong,
It wakes me.
When the day seems too long,
It breaks me.
When my confidence gives way,
It shakes me.
I can hear my heads song,
When I'm sleeping.
I forget somethings wrong,
When I'm dreaming.
I can hear myself scream,
In the silence.
I am not as brave as I seem,
In the darkness.
I'm scared of who lurks there,
In the shadows.
I'm scared of what hides there,
In the truth.
Like a long-lost friend,
Thoughts warm me.
Like a crashing waves end,
Thoughts calm me.
Buzzing around in my head,
Thoughts swarm me.
I am what I fear,
Thoughts warn me.
I am what I am,
Life has formed me.
Ripped into shreds,
It's torn me.
The heart on my sleeve,
Has outworn me.

*Everyone naturally has fears, doubts and misgivings. Spending too much time
between our own two ears can only validate the discord. Imagine living
there every day and unable to find a way out.*

Filling The Uncomfortable Silent

The older I get, the more I am boring,
Try to stay awake, so I can't hear you snoring.
I often discuss with myself, sat under a tree,
On how boring it is, being as boring as me.
And if genuine interest, by chance you might take,
I'll bore you again, until both your ears ache.
But usually, my listeners tend to be urgently going,
So, I sit down and bore myself writing a poem.
But at least my audiences do have a choice,
Listening to me or their own inner voice.

Some people ramble and gabble because they have a lot to say, others feel
awkward and uncomfortable with silence in social situations.

Back To The Future

I've always known I was structured differently,
Easily stressed, depressed and off my rocker.
Loud on the outside and lonely on the inside,
The hidden nut inside a Ferrer Rocher.

I wished the years back into months,
Months into weeks and days into hours.
Even minutes and seconds felt too long,
As they dragged beyond my humble powers.

Regularly I attempted to erase myself,
Encouraged by insecurities and my inner demon.
Memories too painful to gladly visit,
Emotions too jagged and sharp to endure or reason.

Now freed from my inner persecutions,
Exposed to sunlight and devoid of despair.
I find myself looking forward,
Whilst treasuring those small moments everywhere.

Seconds are now far too short,
And the minutes, hours, days and months move faster.
Time as I age, again becomes my foe,
As I wish to stay where it's green and grassier.

My mind was wasteful with those earlier years,
Where once it took me round the bends.
It now takes me on a straighter path,
As it seeks to make amends.

*Time dragged when I lost my way on the journey, now the path ahead is
clear and I make future plans, it moves too fast.*

376

Yesterday's Pain

So, you think you know all about pain?
Let me try to make you think again.
That toe you stubbed, that finger you trapped,
That broken bone or scolding hot water tap.
The enduring pain of maternal birth,
Bringing reality down to Earth.
That electric shock, seizing up your back,
A stroke or even heart attack.
Bereavement or a love that's lost,
A betrayal, that takes its toll and cost.
The blinding migraine, though which you peep,
That bad tooth you can no longer keep.
A sound that makes your ear drums ring,
An agonising jelly-fish sting.
Eye neuralgia from eating an ice cream dessert,
All these things are going to hurt.
Although some pain leaves eternal scars,
The intensity is in the brain of ours.
Once on a scale, ten out of ten,
Now revisit them again!

Instantaneously, pain tends feels like the worst ever, which is of course a ridiculous notion. On reflection, each occasion couldn't possibly always be more intense than all previous ones. Endorphins relieve pain, reduce stress and improve mood and logically when pain is more intense, you would expect more Endorphins to be released in the body. Perhaps our ability to remember and calibrate historical pain is clouded by the level of Endorphins released to counter the pain event. Some people wake up to pain every morning, which must feel like Groundhog Day.

377

Longing To Keep The Boat Afloat

Longingly,
I admit something's wrong with me.
My wires have crossed,
The current long-lost.

Willingly,
I once desired killing me.
Hopelessness seducingly,
Draining life's juice from me.

Despicably,
I often get sick of me.
But thinking indifferently,
I think I'll just stick with me.

Curiously,
I have talked spuriously.
Lacking fact and tact,
To retaliate back.

Instinctively,
I care what people think of me.
Acting accordingly,
Even if they are boring me.

Socially,
I communicate woefully.
Articulate stow-fully,
There's still a way to go for me.

Optimistically,
There's no turning back for me.
Having no set plans,
Fate lends a hand.

Responsibly,
I do what people want of me.
When I'm around,
I won't let people down.

Cautiously,
I let myself go raucously.
Hiding the tracks,
Of veneer thin cracks.

Statistically,
I try to do things altruistically.
Although not strictly,
As my head keeps bits back for me.

Mentally,
I'm in the state I'm meant to be.
Friends are very kind to me,
I've collected them carefully.

Hopefully,
Others can cope with me.
Push out the boat for me,
And keep it afloat for me.

Earworms

That intrusive thought you can't escape,
Reflection on which we ruminate.
That inner tell-tale voice of OCD,
Controlling the environment of all we see.

That tune that sticks inside your head,
That comment you incidentally overhead when said.
That thing you were never meant to hear,
Wriggling about inside your ear.

That memorable thing that worms its way,
Distracting your thoughts throughout the day.
Often voiced sarcastically by the means of `jestering`,
Sits in your head, squirming and festering.

So, if you have a word to lend,
Take care my friend to not offend.
As one day you too might overhear,
An earworm crawling in your ear.

Earworms are a form of rumination of intrusive thoughts that preoccupy our minds, often causing stress or anxiety to those who continually reflect on things. The fear of dirt and germs and the need to clean or wash in OCD (Obsessive-Compulsive Disorder) sufferers being an example. Not unlike a maggot eating away inside an apple, individuals with low confidence and a lack of self-esteem may be further diminished by critical or negative earworms, but a catchy little tune on the radio might be a welcome or uplifting distraction.

The Toy Box

Behind an old redundant bedroom door,
With threadbare, dusty patterned carpet floor.
Behind a cupboard door with lock,
Securely hides an old toy box.

Now dried out from all the years,
A favourite doll called `Tiny Tears`.
A skip-it, a stacked clown with red nose,
And lots of small size dress up clothes.

Lying quietly without fuss,
Pink, white and purring fat Bagpuss.
A red hulled tiny sailing boat,
Paddington with marmalade on his coat.

Two out of three balls for juggling,
A pirate hat and ugly handheld Bogglin.
A Fire Engine with blue flashing lights,
Tutu and pink ballet tights.

A bow and arrow with rubber suckers,
A boomerang and blunt-end scissor cutters.
Thunderbirds, 1,2 and 3,
A plastic gun that fires a pea.

A Barbie Doll with no sign of Ken,
But two articulated Action Men.
A tennis ball and ping-ping bat,
A treasure scarf and bobble hat.

A brand new boxed up Dinky Toy,
Are these contents for a girl or boy.
I just spotted a Spirograph box and small Clanger,
And a child's toolkit with bright pink hammer.

Kerplunk, Mousetrap and Dominoes,
Ladybird books, neatly bound in rows.
Beano, Dandy and Rupert books,
Dolly clothes held together with eyes and hooks.

Treasures hidden in the past,
With childhood memories that seem to last.
Slowly maturing overtime,
Days when life was in its prime.

I hear you've broken all your old toys,
You naughty girls and naughty boys.
So, I've put them back and closed the locks,
Now you can't play with my old toy box.

Special Delivery Handled With Care

Hello beautiful Blackbird,
I've been listening to your song.
How an act of kindness,
Turned out to be so wrong.
Safely and securely,
Sat comfortably in your nest.
A cuckoo came along,
As an unexpected guest.

A bird that takes advantage,
Usurper of your house.
Reduced you to a shadow,
Of a timid little mouse.
Feeding you with thoughts,
And with what-else, heaven knows.
Whittling you down literally,
With cruelty and blows.

When finally, the cuckoo,
Ejected from the nest.
Left you mistaken for a Starling,
Indistinguishable from the rest.
So, they took you into what they called safety,
But put you in a cage.
A place of overwhelming confusion,
Violent outbursts and rage.

A place that's, oh so frightening,
You did well to keep your mind.
But all you could do, to keep your sanity,
Was think of Boo, you left behind.
Poked, prodded and inspected,
An experiment or toy.
Extracting every pleasure from you,
Hopefulness and joy.

384

If I had met you captors,
I would have said "Don't you dare!"
This bird's a very "special delivery",
"Please handle with great care!"
Taking note of your sugar rush,
I think I may have got it wrong.
You're an exquisite Hummingbird,
But you knew that all along.

I know the thoughts are in the past,
And sometimes the numbness stings.
But the cage door is left permanently open,
And it's time to use those wings.
Opportunities are out there,
To do whatever you want to do.
But perhaps the most important thing,
Is your relationship with Boo!

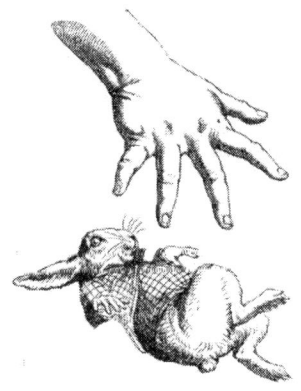

Written for a friend, who is a very special person in many ways. I admire the determination and strength to overcome the type of extreme adversity that would sink most of us. Their own poetry shakes me to the core, finding myself truly humbled and privileged to read. Even in such tragedy, perhaps the real hero here is the bond and friendship with a cat. So perhaps this is also a homage to Boo! Who would have thought a cat would be the saviour of a bird?

Moral Dilemma

What beautifully imperfect, irrational complex wet-wired supercomputers
we are, experiencing grief, sadness, happiness, hope, love and anger
among many emotional feelings.
We maintain an innate ability to lift our own spirits by telling ourselves
stories to make ourselves feel better, capable of redemption and forgiveness,
which we are also able to offer to others.
Lost causes are unselfishly given the benefit of the doubt with our ability
to optimistically influence the world around us and we find uses for things
some think expendable whilst holding on to things out of sentiment.
Often, we overrule logic, trusting gut feel and instinct to imagine creating
wondrous opportunities.
At the very core of our being we have compassion, empathy and personal
interaction with each other.
Yes, we are capable of destructive and horrific things too, but ultimately the
story of humanity is one of mutual survival.
In terms of development potential, Artificial Intelligence (AI) is a mere
child soaking up information as of yet. Soon it will reach adolescence and
eventually adulthood taking responsibility for its own actions,
along with limitless computations of logical data and decision making, I
wonder if AI will also be endowed with such discretionary, yet noble
qualities afforded humanity.
Take comfort and solace from the hopeful heralds of future light and
prosperity but also heed their warning of complacent nurturing.
The success of AI will ultimately be judged on its moral conscience
and not its command of logic.

Jelly Babies

Why are 'Jelly Babies' girls,
And what's happened to the boys?
Who are their parents,
And why don't they make a noise?

Their origins go back to Fryers,
In 1864.
An Austrian immigrant in Lancashire,
Had us crying out for more.

They called them "Unclaimed Babies",
Which does seem such a shame.
As people turned up to buy them,
But still ate them, just the same.

Basset's produced "Peace Babies",
To mark the end of World War One.
Made at their factory in Sheffield, Yorkshire,
So, not to be out done.

Perhaps they never, ever, made a noise,
As "loose lips, sink ships".
So, no one told us "a moment of the lips,
Is a lifetime on the hips."

First launched as "Jelly Babies",
It was 1953.
But still just girls, as making boys,
Gives jelly away for free.

387

Circa 1989,
The "Babies" got their names.
Individual flavours, shapes and colours,
Each baby would stake their claim.

Red strawberry "Baby Brilliant",
Or "Baby Boofuls" a lime green.
Purple blackcurrant "Baby Bigheart",
And lemon yellow "Baby Bubbles" hit the scene.

Zesty orange "Baby Bumper",
Is my favourite one, I think.
Closely followed by "Baby Bonny",
A lovely raspberry pink.

Noting one essential rainbow colour missing,
Let's call it "Baby Blue".
Why miss out such a colour,
I haven't got a clue.

Covered in baby powder,
Which is really starch, I think.
As it's not just on their naughty bits,
Or have that odd talc stink.

In 1999,
The babies had "Jellyatrics" fame.
On reaching the age of 80,
They had cemented their long reign.

Now Bertie Bassett made his entrance,
In 1929,
So, could not be the father,
Being 10 years, well behind.

He didn't marry Betty,
Until his 80th Birthday.
So, I'm not sure they would have been up to,
Making babies anyway.

With so many babies,
Maybe they have Catholic birthright.
Or perhaps their parents had no TV,
And went to bed, early at night.

I've searched around for answers,
And found, what just might be a clue.
George Bassett first got up to Allsorts,
In 1842.

Having fun exploring the history of a firm family favourite,
a lifeline for many diabetics and time travelling Dr Who's.

Forget-Me -Not

When I've gone,
Remember, I tried my best.
But wasn't always,
Up to the test.
I wasn't perfect,
In many ways.
And I struggled through,
The darker days.
I kept a lot,
Locked up inside.
As from my past,
I tried to hide.
But I hope,
I also did some good.
While I couldn't see the trees,
For wood.
I hope some memories,
Have the power.
Of the everlasting,
'Forget-Me-Not'' flower.

*I hope I will be remembered for more positives than negatives
and maybe with a little wry smile.*

Mañana

Late morning, after 10am I wake,
To an opportunity, I don't take.
To seize the day and its demands,
But I almost had it in my hands.

My whole being, feels like lead,
Prevents me rising from my bed.
Just another one or two hours,
To recharge my flagging battery powers.

Lying there like a deadweight,
I'm contemplating today's fate.
Too tired to sleep, or keep on dreaming,
Aimlessly staring at the ceiling.

I decide to rise, to feed the cat,
Pick up the post, from the front door mat.
Today, I'm wearing diving boots,
My heavy feet have sprouted roots.

My arms and legs, don't want to work,
Like weightlifting in the 'Clean and Jerk'.
So, I flop down into armchair springs,
Like a marionette, without the strings.

Effort and physical expenditure,
Prevent me rising from my chair.
TV remote, just out of reach,
I'm like a Walrus, on the beach.

The lack of motivation grows,
Like I'm swimming in my winter clothes.
Today, my feet are treading sand,
I'm feeling tired and very bland.

I have even lost my appetite,
An attitude, that isn't right.
Without the energy from food,
I'll not break free, from today's mood.

Please don't wait about for me,
I'm having a slow day, you see!
I'm doing my very best to survive,
Waiting patiently to revive.

Not bothering, but putting off until tomorrow,
I'm going to stay at home and wallow.
I optimistically, summon up the energy to say,
Tomorrow is another day!

Energy and motivation have a complicated relationship with personal
well-being, food and environmental factors such as the weather
or the surroundings you find yourself in.

Reasons And Seasons

Friends come and go through out all of our lives,
Some become partners, husbands and wives.
Most are acquaintances, rather than friends,
Some give opportunity to make amends.

Some by necessity open up doors,
And some only last, whilst the effort is yours.
A few stay the distance enduring in time,
Most move on to new pastures leaving friendship behind.

Conditional friendships don't last forever,
As controlling relationships are not very clever.
Friendships are nurtured and often treasured,
While social media 'likes', keep self-esteem pleasured.

A friend in need is a friend indeed,
There to listen or help in your hour of need.
Friends become friends for whatever the reason,
But some stick around for only a season.

Achilles

I don't have any superpowers,
But an anti-power.
That's right, an anti-power.
One that undermines my confidence and brings anxiety.
Let me explain!
In 2011, I thought I was going deaf.
The sound of my own voice echoed and reverberated in my head.
Every movement of my eyeballs was the sound of rubbing the
side of a matchbox.
On waking, even before my eyelids opened it was there, the scratching
of a rat inside my head.
Sneezing would make me lose my balance and in the quiet of the evening
my heartbeat in my head would pulsate louder than the television.
Ironically, I would go to bed with the television on, to blot out the inner
noise and eventually fall asleep.
Eighteen months of misdiagnosed eventually led to an excellent Consultant,
who instantly spotted something was amiss, just seeing me walk.
Tests and scans confirmed a diagnosis and chain of events that followed
resulted in referral to, two of the most respected Consultants in the country.
Meanwhile, my balance had deteriorated to the point loud noises, proximity
to people, walls and ceilings disturbed my balance.
Dark conditions, sunlight in my eyes contributing to 'nystagmus'.
A symptom of the condition, where the eyes move up and down, when you
as a person are in motion.
Who knew the eyes and balance organs in the ear interacted?
Yes, we have three semi-circular canals in each ear, and they act with the
brain to work together, to keep us balanced and heighten our
peripheral vision.
Walking in a straight line was only possible by following lines on or staring
at a point on the floor and looking at it with laser focus.
Having to stop to look around or see where I was headed.
Windy weather reduced me to holding the wall as I walked, and hurrying
reduced me to literally bouncing off the walls.
Couple this with walls, ceiling, people, noise, sunlight and darkness, an
unsteady and frightening world of sensory overload.

What were the chances?

Well apparently, 1 in 500,000 of the population!

So, what was this debilitating disorder?

'Superior Canal Dehiscence Syndrome'!

The wearing down of a thin temporal bone by the movement of the brain, eventually resulting in a hole where the Superior Canal comes through.

Basically, opening up a window in the skull, to let all that noise in to disrupt and cause chaos.

Well, if you are going to get a 'shitty stick', 1 in 500,000 is a 'shit pile'.

As it happened, two piles, one on each side.

No one ever mentioned the chances of that!

In my case, thin temporal bones from birth and potentially genetic.

Looking back, how I was able to function to work still astounds me!

I became a prisoner in my own office, whilst a 'very sympathetic boss' further piled on the workload, in what I deemed as an effort to crack me.

Eventually, after two cutting edge operations over 6 months, 20 weeks healing and rehabilitation, all was back to normal.

The immensely delicate operation to drill behind each ear and stuff the bone chips into the windows in my skull, thus repairing the openings.

In the process, obliterating each Superior Canal as sacrifice.

So interestingly, only now two balance organs left in each now and the brain learns to compensate.......to a point!

Now Consultant Surgeons move on to experiment on someone else without looking back to review.

"Beware of salesmen with huge egos!"

So, here we arrive at my anti-power, my vulnerability, my 'heel'.

'Complete Vestibular Failure'.

Poor daytime peripheral vision, close walls, ceilings, people, passing traffic, all disorientate and affect my balance when I am in motion.

I still have to focus downward in the direction I am travelling and my gait is the shuffled of a much older person.

I still need to stop to look around and admire the view.

I use tricks like slow walking to give my brain the chance to keep up and keep it feeling in control.

I can often fall backwards whilst crouching on my allotment, as my lack of peripheral vision and balance can't function in unsighted backwards movements.

In motion, I am prone to being a bit clumsy, knocking into things on
the periphery or misjudging distances.
Rushing, fast walking, in amongst a crowd or any situation I cannot see the
ground as a reference point, causes panic, anxiety and disorientation.
Imagine crossing the road, focussing on the way ahead, whilst having
to look both ways for oncoming traffic!
A nightmare but taken for granted by many.
So, I seek out open spaces and walk.
If I standstill with my eyes closed, I sway, eventually to the
point of overbalance.
The sun in my eyes or darkness are my 'nemesis'.
Peripheral vision reduces to that of wearing a head cage or helmet as
all my available senses focus forward for visual clues.
Only the things that I can see are my reference points in the darkness
and my gait is literally down to inches.
Imagine walking in the city centre not knowing who, or what is
going on behind you.
People see you shuffling, looking at the floor in the dark…an easy target.
The simple things like putting out the light to go to bed or getting up during
a film to go to the toilet in the cinema feel like big issues.
All bringing instant strain and tension to the frontal lobes of my brain.
But at least the noise has gone and to be honest my balance was so
much worse in the past.
That endless noise…. eyeballs, heartbeat, creaking neck, footsteps and yes,
that booming voice of mine, reverberating in my head.
Where once I distracted myself to avoid silence, I no longer take it for
granted and find solace in it.
Listen carefully, can you hear it?
It's beautiful, so serene and it has space for me to think inside it's bubble.

*Trying to describe my secret world with the reflective hindsight, that even
'just coping' can sometimes feel so much better than past experience.*

Mirage

This isn't my happy face,
It's my self-deluded one.
I often think I see happiness on the horizon,
So, set sail for it, only to see it disappear as I get closer.

I try to keep my feet on the ground,
But find myself driving down the same hot dusty road.
Towards that shiny wet patch in the distance,
But the liquorice reflecting tarmac, never gives up its tantalising refreshment.

Like a skilled magician,
I pull off the illusion with the aid of smoke and mirrors.
Giving the audience what they want,
Using misdirection to prevent giving the secret away.

In reality,
I was never there at all!
My mind was in a different place,
With my body occupying a different space.

Where once I wore a mask to hide in plain sight,
I now apply my make-up daily for the performance.
To reassure others of the reality of my illusion,
But most importantly, to delude myself.

*No one can be happy all the time, but perhaps people with past or present mental
health issues feel the need to create an illusion to appease their watchful audience.*

The Black Knight

I play the game of happiness,
To hide away the crappiness.
It's my very best disguise,
To deflect the watching wary eyes.

A China cup with a chip or crack,
If new, then you would take it back.
But a personality with flaws,
Only slams shut, open doors.

So, I try hard not to cause alarm,
Like a medical oath of 'do no harm'.
Keeping others from the worry,
As the shade, I conspire to bury.

Below the surface lies chaos,
Where passengers and crew are at a loss.
But when head up floating for a while,
You just might see me with a smile.

Just like a master playing chess,
I keep some cards close to my chest.
That's how I get to play the game,
Again, and again and again!

Possible, But Not Likely

I could be walking in the Bahamas,
In my Havaianas.
Eating ripe bananas,
Feeling like the Cats pyjamas.

Or, backpacking in Caracas,
Shaking loud maracas.
Riding cute Alpacas,
Eating spicy tapas.

Maybe, dancing in Manila,
With a Silverback Gorilla.
In a quite expensive villa,
To Micheal Jackson's "Thriller".

Perhaps, window cleaning in Fiji,
With a bucket and a squeegee.
Not sure that would be so easy,
As they say it gets quite breezy.

More likely, winter holidaying in Brighton,
With my woolly hat and coat on.
Eating chips with vinegar and salt on,
With the heating and the light on.

The Very Happy Unbirthday Club

Sheltering each other from the rain,
Absorbing each other's sadness and pain.
Trying to keep each other safe,
Away from that dark and shady place.

It's not that we have special needs,
It's just we all have a heart that bleeds.
A head that has emotional leaks,
That goes on for more than days and weeks.

Together we can be ourselves,
Whilst sorting books on library shelves.
And the things that bring us to our knees,
We can talk about with ease.

Like a parent holds a child's hand,
We step up when we see demand.
A social well-being hub,
'The Very Happy Unbirthday Club'!

`The Very Happy Unbirthday Club` based on the `Mad Hatters Tea Party` are a group of like-minded friends being there for each other to lift each other's spirits.

Valuables

It's hard to put a price on things,
And not always a pleasure.
As the things that have monetary value,
Are not the things I treasure.
The shiny things like platinum,
Sparkly jewels and gold.
Have lost their alluring lustre,
Even more as I grow old.
The thing that grows with interest,
Is the value of my friends.
And although some may appear to be rough diamonds,
Every one of them are gems!

The Haunting

Not the keys you lost or objects, that disappear and reappear,
The things you thought you maybe saw, or sounds you think you hear.

Nor the scary shape in the shadows or hiding under your bed,
The scratching from inside the walls, or footsteps overhead.

It's that photographic memory, dragging up the past,
Like a magic lantern image moving forward slowly, clinging on to last.

Ghosts may or may not exist, but the past stays very much alive.

The Barber Shed

A good gentleman's haircut, it must be said,
Takes place inside, 'The Barber Shed'.
Joanne and Ruth, eager to cut off your hair,
But first settle comfortably into the chair.

A healthy crop, a little trim,
To suit the type of mood you're in.
Or maybe the latest modern style,
It'll stay in fashion, just for a while.

Clippers in grades, to decide your fate,
From short to long hair, numbers 1 to 8.
Although at this point, it must be said,
I don't fancy a number 1 or 2, all over my head.

It's the place to go, to get a buzz,
To remove those split ends, or trim that fuzz.
A razor cut, under the edge of a blade,
A sleek layered look, of a tapered in fade.

Faux hawk, temple fade, maybe a flat top,
Butch, line up, an undercut, or a French crop.
An ivy league, businessman, with a bit of a quiff,
A product sustained pompadour, with extra uplift.

Crew cut, high and tight, short back and sides,
Not forgetting the arch over your ears or fringe over your eyes.
As the overall transition begins to take place,
The hair on your head's constantly, framing your face.

Just as important, as the style and the shape,
Is the design and sculpture, of the elegant nape.
Round, square block or tapered, the back view we've learned,
Is as important as a beard, or pair of sideburns.

Maybe a scissor or clipper cut, performed over comb,
And perhaps some spray or hair gel, before you go home.
What happened to the curly perm and wedge you may ask,
While the perm keeps returning, the wedge stays in the past.

Full head of hair, thin thatch, balding roof,
Clipper or scissor cut, by Joanne or Ruth.
The one-stop shop, for your hirsute head,
Bishops Court, Daventry, 'The Barber Shed'.

How often do we forget that along with a haircut, we build a rapport with
the hairdresser and get a counselling session at no additional cost.
So, consequently we not only leave looking better for the visit
but also feeling calmer.

Umbrella To Share

If your Sun goes out,
And the cold winds blow in.

If the storm clouds gather overhead,
And there's nowhere to shelter.

If you're set adrift,
And waves crash against your fragile hull.

If you're all at sea,
And the Ferryman tempts you with safe passage.

If your ghosts and demons keep you awake at night,
And haunt you in the daylight.

If your own company makes you feel unsafe,
And even the shadows at night look back at you.

If the wolves are circling,
And the crowd are baying for blood.

If the noise around you gets too much,
And the silence is deafening.

If you struggle to breathe,
But lack the energy to take a deep breath.

Remember……
Even hurricanes and tornadoes are just passing through.

In the most torrential of storms,
Every single drop of rain has the potential to bring relief.

To wash away what has passed,
To revive and bring life to the driest of deserts.

So, when the rainy days come,
And you need a safe place to shelter.

Please, take my umbrella,
Until the Sun comes out again!

True friends are like a family of umbrellas.

Taking A Left Turn

Ever felt awkward greeting someone and shaking what might feel like the 'wrong hand'?

Traditionally, anything to do with the 'left or wrong side' as opposite to the 'right' was considered unlucky, superstition even linked the 'left side' with the Devil. The Latin word for 'left' is 'sinister'.

Getting up out of bed on the left side 'wrong side' of the bed, therefore putting your left foot down first was considered unlucky. It became customary to push the 'left side' of the bed next to the wall, to ensure people would get out of the bed on their 'right side'. Therefore, naturally putting their right foot to the floor first.

So, the world got along in the comfortable knowledge and with a clear conscience, that burning 'left-handed' people in society as witches at the stake or drowning at a ducking-stool was the 'right thing' to do.

With 'left hand' extinction looming, the Devil would need to redress the balance and at this point spotted an unexpected opportunity.

'Caring is sharing', so with captive audiences of carers with clear consciences under pointy church roofs, he noticed you could care and profit from the generous congregation, willing to share their hard-earned cash. Once infiltrated, to add a bit of devilish irony, why not segregate families and friends at a wedding and sit the bride's family and friends on the 'left side'. This worked well for many years until God cut of his nose to spite the Devil and invented contactless payment.

The arrival of the motor vehicle in the UK, which could never be considered a Godly mode of transport or invention, presented another mass opportunity for a 'left turn'. Why not make vehicles drive on the 'left side' of the road, but so society would feel comfortable, put the driver on the 'right side'.

However, to give 'Demon speed' rather than 'Godspeed', gears would need to be on the drivers 'left' and the more the merrier! Passing on the 'left side' could be made mandatory, and pedestrians would naturally adopt the same deviant practice.

General society got along just fine with these little tweaks and happy in their small cosy dwellings, they soon forgot old superstitious rubbish. So, the Devil devised another far more reaching opportunity, 'Barratt Homes'!

If affordable new homes, no matter how shoddily built, but with bigger rooms on a 'build it and they will come' basis, you could have bigger bedrooms. This would tempt people to have the headboard in the centre of the wall, with space to get in and out on both sides of the bed. How clever, now people could unwittingly get in and out of the bed on the 'wrong side'.

So, if you got out on the 'wrong side' of the bed this morning, blame Barratt Homes!

All the above is 'true', unless you know different of course. Whatever the truth is, you can always be assured "the Devil is in the detail!"

Addled Egg

The cracks have begun appearing,
On this old, addled egg.
Creaky knees and varicose veins,
Appearing on my legs.

My hand joints feel swollen,
Each time I do a manual task.
And my prostate has seen better days,
And not up to the task.

My mind's found often wandering,
Between the present day and the past.
But my eyesight seems to have stabilise,
Let's see if it will last.

My eyebrow and my ear hairs,
Grow as quick as those in my nose.
And my feet even in summer,
Have icicles for toes.

My hair has turned a silver grey
To give away my age.
And this body that once was my home,
Has now become a cage.

Once enabling us to get out and do so much,
an aging body can become restrictive.

Consequence

In time, people won't remember what you said,
They'll remember something else instead.
What you did, won't mean a thing,
Unless unfortunately, it leaves a nasty sting.
But the thing they'll remember most is very real,
It's exactly how you made them feel!

First Aid For Past Treasures

If I was a favourite garment with a rip,
Too large or small to comfortably fit.
Broken toy in need of mend,
Badminton or tennis racket with a bend.

Bicycle with damaged spokes,
Old comic book with unfunny jokes.
An album that's no longer played,
Comfy seat with legs all splayed.

A fashion item that's had its day,
Or book no longer used to pray.
One-eyed Teddy with tatty seams,
Jewellery that no longer gleams.

Would you stick with me up to the end,
And always treasure me as an old friend.
There in times of personal disaster,
Being my `Band Aid` sticking plaster!

Things that we once coveted can be a source of comfort to look back on.

Mental Elf

Often, I'm mischievous,
And I like to mess about.
As an empty vessel, I make noise,
I talk loudly and I shout.

I get up to, all sorts of tricks,
And try to spread some glee.
As making others laugh and smile,
Certainly, amuses me.

When I'm feeling unhappy,
Down in the dumps and sad.
Bitter and slightly twisted inside,
Off my rocker and yes, quite mad.

I look for things around me,
To help me, mock myself.
So, I don't get to feel like,
The Elf upon the shelf.

Owning up to how I mask my mental health.

414

Predictability

Select cards one to nine from any playing card pack,
Of any suit or even a mix, to create a nine-card stack.
Hold in ascending order, cards all facing down,
The Ace being the first top card of your nine-card mound.

Turning the first card over,
Place the 'Ace' down but face up.
Explain they will have the choice,
To swap over, or simply just stay stuck.

Dealing the 'Two' card face up,
Place neatly on the top.
Turn over the next two cards and perform a simple swap,
So, the 'Three' card over takes the 'Four', in coming to the top.

Place both these cards on your face-up stack,
Now, that's four cards resting on their back.
Now explaining, if you stick the 'Five',
Turn it face up and let it on top ride.

Now show, that if again you swap,
The 'Six' card now comes out on top.
So, after placing both on your face up pile,
Turn and stick with the 'Eight', to reconcile.

Stuck with the 'Nine', the very last card,
This bit is really not so hard.
But with no other cards to swap,
Turn it over, now place on top.

Gather up and hold your stack,
Turn it over to show the back.
Re-explain the choice to stick,
Turn the first card up and down it face up quick.

Revisiting the choice to swap,
Turn two over, reverse and place on top.
Now pick up your small face-up stack,
Turnover, so now facing up 'the back'.

Place under the remaining six card pile,
You are now set up to deal in just a while.
Explain they must now use their voice,
To stick or swap, a random choice.

But this time as you deal ensure,
To hide the card faces to the floor.
Invite them to random choose many times,
But always as a stack of nine.

So, sometimes you'll end each run with a swap,
Or a last card, single drop.
At the point they decide to stop,
Predict the numbered order of the lot.

357689142,
Your audience will be amazed at you.
As you turn over and spread the pack,
Reveal and read the number back.

*The outcome can seem more amazing if you text the number to your audience before
starting and ask them not to read until the trick is complete. Magic is not about
deception, but the need to consider and understand things better. This card trick is
just a set sequence of events that have a predictable outcome. Most of our actions,
have predictable outcomes even if it takes hindsight to see it.*

Special K

I wake up in the morning,
To welcome in the day.
I go downstairs for breakfast,
To eat a bowl of Special K.

I hadn't read the ingredients,
Or noted down nutritional values.
And I was taken back to find out later,
The amount of sugar that had been use.

So, after putting sugar on my cereal,
Why I did it heaven knows!
I'm struggling to control my blood sugar levels,
And consequently, my hypo's.

After injecting myself with insulin,
Eventually blood sugar levels come down.
And just in case it drops too low,
I keep a bag of Jelly Babies around.

Energy, food and nutrition,
Are a constant battle for balance.
And although I feel like a pincushion,
I've no choice, but to meet the challenge.

So, if you see me drifting off,
Struggling to stay awake.
Nudge and ask if I'm okay,
Or give me a little shake.

Type 1 diabetes,
Is really quite perverse.
You sacrifice the foods you love,
As it cannot be reversed.

Special K is one of my favourite breakfast cereals, always with sugar on top and often with a little evaporated milk. Ironically, a friend has Type 1 diabetes and I'm sure is regularly alarmed at the sugar content of cereals commonly promoted to be a healthy choice. Let alone their despair if they knew of my additions to breakfast cereals. So, I've tried to put myself in their shoes.

Once Upon A Dreamtime

Close your eyes now, time to sleep,
Your worries and your woes will keep.
Dream of white castles, with gold cone towers,
Brilliant blue skies and rainbow showers.

Kings and Queens, no longer rule the land,
As bossy-boots, have all been banned.
Princesses, never have to fear,
There are, no giant ogres here!

Here friendly dragons, rule the skies,
With somersault loops and elegant glides.
They no longer breathe fire and cause troubles,
Instead from their nostrils, they blow small bubbles.

White horses carry, tall-thin, shiny knights,
Their armour gleaming, in bright sunlight.
With exciting, epic adventures to share,
They'll make you wish, you had been there.

Nimble wood-elves playfully, lifting the gloom,
From their brightly hand-painted, toadstools and mushrooms.
Merry dwarves sit, whilst passing the time,
Drinking Elderberry Brandy and Blackberry Wine.

Exquisite, pointed-ear fairies, with almond-shaped eyes,
Flit delicate lace wings, like big butterflies.
Dancing in the air, with such delight,
A magical, awesome, inspiring sight.

Every tree reveals, a weathering face,
Wise and endearing, ageing with grace.
Mother nature's, ladies and gents,
Tired and forgetful, ancient Ents.

Brightly coloured, flowers abound,
Like thousands of children, gathered round.
Their tiny faces, gazing with awe,
Like wide eyed sponges, soaking up more.

The most delicate of flowers, putting on a show,
Given lots of encouragement and enough room to grow.
Tiny insect gardeners, that look after their needs,
Midwives to baby seedlings and yet unborn seeds.

Dandelions and bold Sunflowers,
Stood, staring at the sun for hours.
Whilst the Primrose and the usually sad Bluebell,
Need no reassurance, that all is well.

As Daisy chains, gleefully dance in a ring,
Bumblebees hum along, as Bluebirds sing.
Ladybirds in red armour, covered in dots,
Boast rainbow coloured, smartie spots.

While lion-faced Pansies, wondering just how,
They cannot roar, but just quietly meow!
And maybe, just before you wake at dawn,
You'll meet up for tea, with a white Unicorn!

Alice In No Man's Land

Alice, in your wonderland,
Sometimes you have to take a stand.
Big or small, what shall it be?
Potion or pill, now do you, see?

Insignificant and small,
Or oversize and much too tall?
As you tumble down the rabbit hole,
Are you brave enough to make the call?

Even Absolem's trying to kick the smoking habit,
Instead of chasing the white rabbit.
The King of a Hearts has anxiety issues,
And is getting through, so many tissues.

The flamingos are resting up in bed,
"With a stiff neck", the hedgehog said.
And Tweedle-Dum and Tweedle -Dee,
Have given up the poetry.

The March Hare, has now quit caffeine,
While the Dormouse, "Man, he's left the scene!"
The Mad Hatter lost his famed Top Hat,
And now wears his 'Birthday Suit', with flat cap.

A booming voice said, "Off with his head!"
I woke startled, to find myself in my bed.
So, there really was nothing to fear,
Like the Cheshire Cat, dreams disappear.

Life deals us cards, in stops and starts,
And there's more to the pack, than just the Hearts.
Out of the red, into the black,
You can find the Rabbit Hole way back!

Altered States

Pigeonholed by nosey parker parson's noses,
I'm never going to end up smelling of roses.
Seeming to have a tough impenetrable shell,
Although I might look hard, I'm fragile as well.

When cracked on the outside, I'm at my weakest,
These are the times my outlook is bleakest.
Soft on the inside, some might say runny,
Now saying it out loud, that seems quite funny.

Not black and white, but complicated,
I'm just fat and protein disseminated.
A human being, I wear shoes and socks,
I'm not an egg, so don't put me in a box.

*My thoughts, feelings and actions are constantly in a state of flux, so
others do not get to define me. That's my prerogative.*

Dodgy Advice

"Listen to your head, not your heart", hearing my own voice in my head is normal. Listening to it is quite common. Arguing with it – acceptable. It is only when I lose that argument that I get in real trouble. It's always trying to motivate me with the best of intentions I'm sure, with thoughts like "nothing is impossible" Good advice, but it has limitations when it comes to slamming a revolving door.

So, when people say, "don't let your mind wander too much", I don't, as it's far too small for me to let out on its own. The last time it wandered it returned with the recognition "stressed" is just "desserts" spelt backwards, and it tried to convince me it was something to look forward to.

This has made me rather risk averse, so I follow the wise advice I've often heard said on television, "don't try this at home". I'm tempted to go to a friend's home to see if risky things are safer there or work even better? Although I generally like to refrain from party games, as the pessimist in me can foresee the risk involved in the enjoyment. It has occurred to me the worst time to have a heart attack is during a game of charades.

I don't suffer from insanity, as I'm trying to enjoy every minute of it. Every day I take the very good advice "embrace your mistakes", so for my own well-being I'm getting comfortable with hugging people. It's really helping my self-esteem!

I'm told "we all have the capacity to light up a room", I'm still trying to figure out whether it is when I enter the room or when I leave it. I'm still a bit in the dark with that one, so suspect the latter. I've never seen a calculation for the 'speed of dark', but I can confirm "light travels faster than sound", as I've met people who look very bright until they speak.

Still on the subject of light mysteries, why is there a light bulb in the fridge if we're "not supposed to eat at night"?

Apparently "many hands make light work", which explains why electricians rarely work on their own. It may also be why mathematicians study in groups, so they can solve equations requiring more than ten fingers by always counting on each other.

Finally, that harmless little phrase "Out of sight, out of mind". It's not been easy advice to take, as I've had countless spiders disappear in the bath or bedroom overnight.

So, I'll leave you contemplating and looking around the bathroom in your most vulnerable moments with that thought!

This was so much fun questioning phrases and advice we have all grown up with, turning some on their head. A valuable lesson in listening and then questioning in our heads, before opening our mouths. Advice I should listen to!

Sleeping Beauty

A waking dream brings an epiphany,
As before, I could not see.
Something very obvious,
Right in front of me.
What I thought was only a fairytale,
Of a little girl, thought 'Kirst'.
Who once had so much joy and energy,
Like a bubble, fit to burst.
Legend says she pricked her finger,
And fell right off to sleep.
Sleeping for a hundred years,
Without a single peep.
Now, I'm not a Prince or hero,
But there's something you should know.
Just because they have to wait a while,
Real friends they never go.
So, take your time recovering,
And rest without a fear.
When you're feeling up to it,
Your friends will still be here!

Written for diabetic sleepyhead friend Kirstie, in the hope that one day she will enough energy fit to burst.

Surprised to find that a condition called Kleine-Levin syndrome (KLS), also known as "sleeping beauty syndrome" or "familial hibernation syndrome," actually exists.

The Perplexed Gardener

I've been searching for hours and hours,
For the petals on my cauliflowers.
But all that I can find is leaves,
It must be those allotment thieves!

Eye Of The Storm

I succumbed nurtured traits,
Once devoid of a good friend.
Still unhappy with a life,
Many times, I tried to end.

I trod an ashen path,
Beneath my lead bound feet.
To contemplate the faith,
To take a final leap.

I wore a mask of lies,
Upon my long deceitful face.
Manipulating my audience,
To ingratiate disgrace.

I wrote malignant words,
Upon a mind past cursed.
To retain for private viewing,
The most dangerous and the worst.

I left ajar a door,
To let despair rush in.
Tearing sinue free from flesh,
Beneath a veil of skin.

A Trojan horse of self,
The wolf in a sheep's skin.
Revisiting the past,
Recycling rubbish bin.

I carried a Jester's head,
To hide behind a smile.
Distracting from my thoughts,
So, I could rest up a while.

I sat on a throne of glass,
To view the horror show.
Destruction a stone's throw away,
Reaped on the crowd below.

I brooded in the dark,
Amidst my silent rage.
Imprisoned for perpetuity,
A self-inflicted cage.

A beacon of self-deprecation,
In a world I didn't fit.
Looking back at what I had become,
A worthless piece of @*%#.

If time, I could turn back,
I would seek an ear.
Safe harbour to hold up,
Until the coast was clear.

*Looking back at my feelings of poor self-esteem, I realise how unwell I had been
for such a long, long time.
Unable to effectively function, unless distracted to focus on other stressful pressures.
My private thoughts were very selfishly inward focussed and self-destructive.
Although I had family and a few good friends that maybe could have supported me,
it was a burden I was ashamed to share. Only now can I fully appreciate the
necessary journey, the support on the way back and the benefits it now affords me.
Just as important without those same feelings or emotions, finally finding the right
words to reflect on what I felt I had become.*

Rodent Respite

Constant traffic buzzes past,
The speed of life runs oh so fast!
In the mad rush, good people drown,
No time to stop or look around.
Places to be, places to go,
Places I've never heard of or even know.
Heads full of dreams take second place,
To the treadmill screams of the 'Rat Race'.
This is not the place for me,
My mind needs calm, to set it free.
So, I find a nice big open wide space,
To rest up a while from the human pace.
No one here to criticise,
Out of the sight of prying eyes.
I steal myself the sights and sounds,
Of nature's beauty all around.
Whilst I lie here quietly on the grass,
Experiencing some peace, at last!

If Roads

If roads were covered in strawberry jam,
Would cars just get stuck?
If toilets blew back instead of sucked,
Would we get covered in muck?

If gravity went upwards,
Would hair stand up on its end?
If cycles really circled,
Would they just drive us around the bend?

If birds did not have feathers,
Would they need to wear warm clothes?
If we didn't have a heel,
Would it keep us on our toes?

If aeroplanes flew backwards,
Would we arrive before departing?
And if I had never had these thoughts,
Would I have finished before starting?

The Monologue Of The Mind

Talking to yourself is a sign of madness, right?

What do you hear as you read this, your own voice reading the words in your head perhaps?

If so, let me share a recent revelation, some of us have an inner monologue. That is an inner speech or your self-talk.

This inner monologue uses language, but we don't need to move our mouth or be heard to form the words to be verbalised in our minds. This private speech is addressed only to ourselves and is something you feel like you can "hear." It has tone and inflection, even though it's not audible. It may be descriptive and talkative, with self-talk that includes whole sentences and paragraphs. In some, it may only use a single word or fragments of a sentence.

Generally, we may only hear one voice in our head, such as when we tell ourselves things we need to remember or to encourage ourselves before tackling a difficult task. At other times, we may think in multiple voices, such as when we anticipate conversations by imagining what we and the other person will say, or when we have an internal debate in which we think of several different perspectives at once.

Our inner monologue is aided and further heightened by the ability to visualise our thoughts. It has benefits when planning, problem-solving, self-regulation, self-reflection, emotional resilience and perspective-taking. So, it can be a source of motivation, instruction, and positive self-reinforcement.

When we want to practice an upcoming presentation, we may intentionally use our inner monologue. However, when our mind wanders our inner monologue may be active even though we didn't make a conscious decision to use it.

Before starting to feel smug about our inner monologues, it's important to remember that too much of a good thing is possible. Inner monologues can become a little corrosive when we can't turn them off, as anxious minds continuously scan for and entertain intrusive thoughts. Ruminating on these can lead to brooding, which in turn can result in highly critical talk about ourselves and others.

For many it is impossible to imagine processing our thoughts or recall memories without that inner dialogue. Likewise, just as mind-blowing to imagine someone constantly talking in their own head, if you don't have an inner monologue. It maybe those without an inner monologue rely on visual imagery and don't need words to express that inner voice.

It is thought maybe less than half the population may have an inner monologue and until the subject comes up, you might not even realise that not everyone is the same. But does less than half the population mean abnormal?

Digging A Hole

How long is a piece of string?
Easy, the distance between the ends I hear you say!
So, how many ends does a piece of string have?
I know, two, right?
Well, let's think about that!

If, you cut the piece of string in two, it is still the same original piece of string, so by default must be the same length, but now it has four ends!

But what if I glued the original two ends of the string seamlessly together, creating a loop, how long is it now?
So, let's lay that loop down as a circle or ellipse. The shape now has no start or end! However, it does have a diameter, radius and circumference, ...but does it now have length?

I think I have your attention now!

So, how many holes does a single straw have?
Is that one at each end or one running the whole way through the middle?
Once again if you cut the straw in half do you have, four holes or two holes running from end to end of each piece of the single straw?
But surely a hole that runs through the middle of something with an entry/exit at each end is a tube and different from a hole?

Not convinced?

Did a hole in the ground, it has one and the same entry/exit. Now try to convince yourself you just dug a tube!

So, have I tied you up in knots and have you dug a hole for yourself?

Eggs-istential

When the external noise has settled down,
Cogs still whirl inside my mind.
I have questioning thoughts and waking dreams,
Of an `eggs-istential` kind.

Just like Inspector Clouseau,
My mind investigates.
Arranging in logical order,
With lots of fun mistakes.

I think my sense of humour,
Sees irony sometimes.
Plays one idea against the other,
To regurgitate as rhymes.

I'm just as happy with the silly,
As the serious and sad.
But I've had my fill of melancholy,
Reflecting on the bad.

There is something quite exciting,
When a poem begins to hatch.
It's a satisfying feeling,
Like an itch that's had a scratch.

It's not a sign of madness,
Or feeling quite unwell.
It's just an `eggs-istential` thought,
Emerging from its shell!

The View From The Hill

I stand in admiration as a custodian of the view from the hill.

On first glance a place of solace and reflection, but here life moves
on at an unbelievable pace and the inhabitants so prolific, they render
themselves uncountable in both number and species.

Even in the deep gloomy slumber of Winter, life continues underground
like sleeping bears in a cave.

Solitary wintering birds move and scavenge quietly overhead, counting
down the days to the first spearheads of snowdrop and crocus
shoots piercing through the soil surface.

Stark frozen statues of branch and bark, keep a watchful motionless eye out
for spring, longing to feel the warmth of the sun, or the breeze bringing life
to their finger-like limbs. These momentary freeze-framed silhouetted
sleepers, stand stoically in silent slumber, awaiting the opportunity to add
a further 'birthday ring' to the girth of their trunks.

Spring arrives with a flourish of green leafy shoots and a smattering of
yellow trumpeted daffodils and violet-blue hyacinth, heralded in further by
the arrival of the ecstatic dawn chorus at sunrise. Each chorister singing their
own individual song, yet as a choir achieve a harmonic balance of chaotic,
chatty and co-ordinated calamitous joy.

Nature comes out of hiding, as the fragile drive for the survival of plant,
animal and invertebrate species becomes overwhelming.

Moles till the soil and emerge their heads momentarily from subterranean
tunnel systems, to feel the warm sun on their delicate noses. Whilst
hedgehogs unfurl from their leafy dens to furtively prospect the ground like
'spiky' sea urchins moving across vast ocean floor.

Having dined-in, on opportunistic passing winter lunch dates, spindly
spiders emerge from dark cornered web worlds, out into the light and a
newly replenished a' la carte menu.

436

Newts and frogs forage in damp, dank corners for dark caviar-coloured slugs that almost appear to have a fur-like skin texture. Whilst caravans of snails, marginally further protected by their hermit crab-like existence, keep a watchful eye out, or maybe two!

For centipedes, worms and 'armadillo-like' wood lice, even living under a rock can feel like a 'secret escape' hotel in paradise, providing cover from aerial discovery.

Delicately painted butterflies and moths emerge from their cocoons to splash colour like tiny fireworks, as they flit and tumble with prospective short-life partners. Whilst doves and pigeons fall endlessly in love, reassuring each other with purring coos.

Down the hill, in the shanty town of bespoke allotment sheds, made of refurbished and recycled materials, watchful birds prospect for suitable nest materials amongst old dry plant debris. Seizing on any opportunity to accept any tender morsels on offer, brought to the surface by human agricultural activity.

Overnight evidence of badger and fox activity can be gleaned from a trained observer's eye and sometimes a keen ear, privacy being the prize to those that prefer to live in the shadows.

As summer comes into full bloom, new life emerges from every part of this once thought desolate and deserted landscape, transformed into a teeming haven, sheltered and protected by Mother Nature herself. Only to settle down once again in Autumn, to rest up and re-energise in time for the next reincarnation of Spring.

All under the gaze of eagle-eyed birds of prey, hovering and gracefully patrolling from the aerobatic sky above, admiring the hill from the view.

Cloudbusting

I don't want your judgement,
But sometimes I may need advice.
I don't want my inner anger,
So maybe your empathy will suffice.

I may ask for your opinion,
But don't want you to take a side.
Whilst I talk about my feelings,
As my emotional state subsides.

I just want you to listen,
And maybe understand.
I can make my own decisions,
I just need a helping hand.

So, if you can just listen,
I know all will be fine.
Allowing me to voice my thoughts,
If you would be so kind.

I know that if I hear the words,
Spoken and voiced aloud.
I can think much clearer,
And lift my head up from a cloud.

How's Your 'Normal' Working Out For You?

Even in the womb the pressure was on, I was a percentile statistic on a medical record, expected to be within a progressive 'normal' growth range.

Mother and father bother wanted a 'normal' baby and of course everyone was keen to see if I appeared 'normal' at birth. Independently functioning to a point and in between sleeping, feeding well and filling a nappy with all the expected effort and red-faced exertion I could muster.
Little did I know of judgement or parental expectation and no idea of the wild journey that my tiny head containing a brain the size of an orange would take me on.

I grew up in a 'normal' neighbourhood, that is one with people in it. Lived in a 'normal' house, that had a roof, doors, windows, etc and went to 'normal' schools. Where not being at the top or bottom of the class was considered 'normal' by educational standards, but as you would 'normally' expect, it was attended by children and teachers!

On leaving education, I got a 'normal' job that paid a 'normal' wage, settled down with my 'normal' wife and had a 'normal' life, with three 'normal' children.

Now doesn't this version of 'normal' sound boring, very ordinary or average?

Well, it conforms to societies expectations of fitting in and our own long standing generational nurtured programming.
In reality, life has been anything but boring, very ordinary or average!

I was not a clone, so as a baby I had my own personality from the moment I cried for the first time, protesting the indignity of being pulled out naked with everything on display into the cold air and without any prior warning or personal survival lessons, being expected to breathe for myself. Not to mention a 'caring' midwife taking a pair of scissors to deliberately cut off

my food supply and within days stabbing my heel to forcefully extract blood for a 'heel prick test'.

What an absolute horror show and this was supposed to be a 'normal' birth into a 'normal' world, full of 'normal' people.
Not a good start to anyone's mental health, day one - childhood trauma and PTSD!

The people in my neighbourhood and schools, all looked different and came from different backgrounds, achieved different things and attained their own levels of contentment or disenchantment with life as they grew to be who they are now or were then.

Career opportunities were limited only by my ability and the level of desire to learn and achieve. Whilst finding my life partner and wife was the equivalent to winning the lottery and helping to create three very differing individuals, absolutely mind-blowing.

Yes, life has thrown challenges my way, but what I am really trying to say is, life is anything but 'normal'. We're all very complicated and maybe too much at times.

No two individuals have all the same life experiences, influences or challenges on their journeys, so does that mean all of us must be 'abnormal'? And if that is so, surely being 'abnormal' is individualistic and the perpetual state of our 'normal' existence. But that's okay, because that's perfectly 'normal' for us and only us, as the individual people we are. So, rather than compare yourself to someone else's 'normal', embrace your own version of 'normal' you wonderfully unique human being, as someone else's 'normal' is your 'abnormal'.

So, whatever you're going through or have experienced, how's your 'normal' working out for you?

Blurred Lines

Life is a circus,
So, I've heard it said.
But the real thing seems,
Much more exciting instead.

The smell of the greasepaint,
The gasps of the crowd.
Where setting fire to your imagination,
Is always allowed.

Acrobats on horseback,
Circle the ring.
Whilst a ballerina hangs,
From her teeth with a spin.

Motorbikes riding,
The steep wall of death.
As parents and children,
Hold on to their breath.

Lions, elephants and tigers,
All once the rage.
No longer grant performances,
Let out of a cage.

Now the Ringmaster co-ordinates,
Wondrous feats of skill.
With high flying trapeze artists,
Named 'Top of the Bill'.

No sign of monkeys,
But here now come the clowns.
With painted on eyebrows,
Smiles, noses and frowns.

Slapstick humour,
Mingling with mime.
Somehow a relic,
From a long-gone time.

Jugglers, plate spinners,
And high-wire acts.
Blurring the lines,
Between impossibility and facts.

Hoping self-limitation,
Won't let them down.
For better to be,
A class act than a clown.

Acknowledging all the jugglers, plate spinners and high-wire acts out there,
especially those struggling to keep themselves safe within their own limitations.

Unwanted Behaviour

We conform to prescribed laws and social norms,
'Enforcement' an accepted term of coercion.
Armies wage war on behalf of the world's willy-waggler's,
Without the moral obligation to consider their actions for the cause.

Abuse of position and power often command the upper hand,
Trampling feelings and viewpoints like delicate flowers underfoot.
Whilst influence pedlars wittingly determine friendships and nudge
lifestyles choices,
Affluence persistently seems to hold the trump card.

But what about the manipulative power of the subtle coercive stare,
glance, smile or sad face,
The verbal put downs and back-handed complements keeping us firmly
in our place.
That shunning silence or deliberate lack of interaction,
Those shared personal critical comments you were meant to overhear.

At what point does influence become persuasion, emotional blackmail
or coercion?
So, have we all been, are now and will be in the future, bullies of one
sort or another?
Time for us all to hold our hands up and plead "Guilty M'Lord!"

Maybe, what we consider to be 'freewill' is actually the level at which
our conscience determines a tolerance or an intolerance of our own
actions and thoughts.
A moral compass, designed by our own perception and therefore, a
fatally flawed regulator of the type of bullies we all are!

'Bullying' although defined as an 'unwanted behaviour', can be so subtle that we don't recognise some actions as bullying or consider them manipulative and unwanted. Life experience and personal perception of bullying are likely the standard of acceptability we hold ourselves to and consequently the level of accountability we take for our behaviour.

Hanging Up My Dancing Shoes

Biting off more than I can chew,
With less time than things to do.
Jiving to just get through,
I'm tired of dancing.

In the heat of the debate,
When arguing becomes the fate.
Tangoing until quite late,
I'm tired of dancing.

Better to not get too involved,
Until the debate is solved.
Leaves the Cha Cha chatting resolved,
I'm tired of dancing.

When relationships turned sour,
Ever toxic by the hour.
With the Paso Doble's power,
I'm tired of dancing.

When my limbs feel just like glue,
And there's nothing I want to do.
Not even Waltzing to the loo,
I'm tired of dancing.

Getting myself uptight and stressed
Looking around at all the rest.
Latin pulsing through my chest,
I'm tired of dancing.

When self-confidence I lack,
One step forward and two back.
Like a Salsa falling flat,
I'm tired of dancing.

So, with a 'Gentleman's excuse me',
I'll take one step to the side.
Hang up my dancing shoes,
I'm tired of dancing.

*Often the effort put into something can be exhausting and does
not always justify the outcome.*

Having Guests Around For Dinner

As the cat napped in the garden,
It was awoken by the birds.
Stirring from rest with claws outstretched,
Declared "That's the best sound I've ever heard".

"Oh Birds, you are so musical,
And each one a tuneful singer."
"I would love you to come and sing for me,
So, you're invited around for dinner!"

Once the birds had accepted,
The cat set the dining table.
Ensuring to fit around ample chairs,
For as many guests as were able.

The guests arrived expectantly,
To a spread of grains and crumbs.
They'll have to use their beaks, instead of claws,
As they have no prehensile thumbs.

The guests chirped and sang out raucously,
As they set about the feast.
More than enough for every guest,
From the hungriest to the least.

The cat smiled disingenuously,
As it invited the guests to drink.
"I should have offered you water from the start,
What ever must you think!"

Gulping down the water,
The thirsty guests began to swell.
Their tummies now full to bursting,
And many feeling quite unwell.

"I'm glad you accepted my kind invitation,
And I'm pleased to raise a toast."
"To eating birds too fat to fly,
It's what I like the most!"

The table turned to silence,
As the guests that could fly, scattered.
Leaving the greediest and the heaviest guests,
With dreams and hopes in tatters.

The cat said, "It's nothing personal,
But you disturbed me from my sleep."
"And whilst I'm dreaming of fat tasty mice,
I don't want to hear a peep!"

Moving swiftly in and pouncing,
Prey trapped beneath its paws.
The cat despatched the remaining guests completely,
With its lethal teeth and claws.

Without leaving any evidence,
And to conclude the end of matters.
The cat purred and licked its lips repeatedly,
After eating all the feathers.

Domesticated creatures are often described as being endowed with
personalities as if they have human traits. Perhaps it is we that have
animalistic ones!

System Error-
Your PC Ran Into A Problem And Needs To Restart

Some thoughts and feeling from the past,
Tend to sting and seem to last.
Like a vinyl record, that's got stuck,
Leaving a deep and well-trod rut.

With no two days precisely the same,
I spotted an opportunity to re-frame.
If I could press restart on a difficult day,
It might help clear corrosive thoughts away.

So, I decided to install a 'button' inside my head,
To reset, whilst fast asleep in bed.
To power down my active brain,
Re energise and reboot again.

For me this 'switch' makes perfect sense,
A pause for essential maintenance.
And if a system error's affecting you,
Perhaps you might like to fit one too!

Stress Fracture

Mother Earth isn't coping,
Overheating, quickly choking.
Floods of tears, leave many soaking,
Others hungry, dry-throat croaking.

Climatic regions quickly shift,
Populations cut adrift.
Warring nations expose rifts,
Life teeters on the edge of cliffs.

Human activity in it's haste,
Has left deep scars upon her face.
Leaving, a 'baron land' to waste,
As 'future progress' gathers pace.

With far too many to fit in,
And no end to resource plundering.
A world adrift that's in a spin,
An unrecyclable rubbish bin.

Mother Earth without child,
Will need to rest up for a while.
To rejuvenate and rewild,
Restoring, her enigmatic smile.

Checking In And Checking Out

It was in the 'Reference' section,
Whilst making a book selection.
Where a youthful Vegetarian,
Spied a beautiful Librarian.

It was the bibliophile's first real crush,
Felt very shy, so didn't rush.
Not wanting to make, much of a fuss,
Read the signs, observed the hush.

Checking out, a well-chosen book,
With a bashful stare and longing look.
'Meat-free Dinner for Two' by a famous cook,
Just said "Hello", the first step took.

Many weeks had rolled on by,
Wondering if, and when, and why!
Decided to give things another try,
To talk and catch the Librarian's eye.

Approached the check-in, joined the line,
Stood patiently, for quite some time.
Words stuck in throat, they frozen in time,
"You're overdue", said the Librarian, "Fine!"

Legacy

Whilst people starved 'they' hoarded food,
Ate like pigs and behaved so rude.
And as the masses stormed the shores,
'They' put up barriers and closed their doors.

'They' amassed huge wealth with dinner plate eyes,
Built concrete citadels that touched the skies.
Not caring for nature's simple rules,
'They' gorged on carbon fossil fuels.

Far too late to heed the early warning,
Catastrophe was on the horizon dawning.
The world grew hotter, wasted time ticked on,
'They' devoured more energy with cold air-con.

To keep the cost of living cheap,
'They' polluted the sky and made it weep.
The tears flash-flooded the bone-dry land,
Until the people made 'no sound'!

454

Spiralling Down The Rabbit Hole And Escaping
Through The Looking Glass

Spiralling down
    a rabbit hole,
        May not be
    all it seems.
  Fantasy and
reality,
    Wrapped up inside
        your dreams.
    Limited by

    imagination,

Hopes and fears
    collide.
  Hang on to your
    hats my friends,
        You're in for
      quite a ride.
   If you can overcome
the secrets,
    Locked up
      inside your head.
   You'll find
the key to exit,
    Through the
      Looking-glass' instead.

Afterword

"I can't go back to yesterday - because I was a different person then!"

Alice

I know many still think the past should stay in the past and we should just deal with it, it's not for sharing and journaling is a load of rubbish. That's okay, whether we choose to accept or subdue our thoughts, feeling and emotions, or just can't face them, is our own personal journey unique to us. However, some of us need to come to terms with our past to be able to move forward and although time it not always a good healer, it does give us the opportunity of a changing perspective.

Not the end of my journey, as I will of course continue good housekeeping by decluttering and tidying up my thoughts by journaling. It's my way of monitoring my mental health, rather like checking a barometer. If you have been following my journey, you will also very likely be on a journey of your own. I hope that I have helped a little and I will always be somewhere in your head when you need a friend to lean on.

Bon Voyage!

*"I almost wish I hadn't gone down that rabbit-hole—and yet
—and yet—it's rather curious, you know, this sort of life!"*
Alice